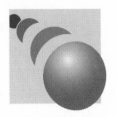

O U G H T E N
H O U S E
PUBLICATIONS

"Books and Tools for the Rising Planetary Consciousness"

Also available ...

Julianne Everett has created five audio tapes: *Ascension Merkabah*, *Soul Alignment*, *Solar Initiation*, *Cellular Transformation*, and *Cosmic Union*. The first tape assists one in creating a vehicle for sustaining the Christ frequency. *Soul Alignment* provides effective tools for healing the past. *Solar Initiation* is a gift from the initiators of the Christ within, including Sananda, Mother Mary, Lord Maitreya, and Lady Kwan Yin. *Cellular Transformation* provides tools for releasing limiting belief systems that may still be recorded within and around your body. *Cosmic Union* is designed to accelerate the ascension process by preparing the physical, emotional, mental, and etheric bodies to receive more of the Holy Spirit.

These tapes can be ordered from Oughten House Publications at the address shown on page 224.

HEART INITIATION

Preparing for Conscious Ascension

by

Julianne Everett

Editing, Typography, and Design by Sara Benjamin-Rhodes

Published by

OUGHTEN HOUSE PUBLICATIONS

Livermore, California USA

HEART INITIATION
PREPARING FOR CONSCIOUS ASCENSION

COVER ART BY ANDRÉE R. ORECK

EDITING, TYPOGRAPHY & DESIGN BY SARA BENJAMIN-RHODES

Published by:
Oughten House Publications
P.O. Box 2008
Livermore, California, 94551-2008 USA

Library of Congress Cataloging-in-Publication Data
Everett, Julianne.
Heart Initiation : preparing for conscious ascension / by Julianne Everett. --
   2nd ed.

        p.   cm.
   Includes bilbiographical references
   ISBN 1-880666-36-7 : (alk. paper)
    1. Spirit writings. 2. Channeling (Spiritualism). 3. Spiritual life--
Miscellanea. 4. Self--Miscellanea. 5. Ascended masters. I. Title.
BF1290.E94   1996
299' .93--dc20   96-52582
                                 CIP

ISBN 1-880666-36-7, Trade Paperback

Printed in United States of America
Printed with vegetable ink on 100% recycled acid-free paper

TABLE OF CONTENTS

(continued)

❧ Acknowledgments ❧

To my beloved life mate, Wally, for his patience
and loving companionship in getting this to press.

To Sara Benjamin-Rhodes, the editor of this second edition, for her
amazing insight and dedication to excellence, and to my publisher,
Oughten House, for supporting my service in the world.

To the omnipresent Spiritual Hierarchy,
for all of their assistance in helping me
to understand that the ascension
is a glorious, ongoing process.

and

To all of the beloved souls who are
consciously working to bring our planet
and her people into ever-increasing levels
of unconditional Love and unlimited Light!

❧ Publisher's Note ❧

We at Oughten House extend our wholehearted appreciation and gratitude to each of our Literary Producers for making this publication possible: Marge and John Melanson, Barbara Rawles, Robin Drew, Irit Levy, Debbie Detwiler, Kiyo Monro, Alice Tang, Eugene P. Tang, Brad Clarke, Victor Beasley, Ruth Dutra, Nicole Christine, Dennis Donahue, Fred J. Tremblay, Kathy Cook, and Debbie Soucek.

❧ The Vision ❧

As I prayed "Almighty, indwelling God, heal,"

I became two: my self and my God-self.

My God-self looking at me,

Looking from Creation's doorway,

Silently acknowledging my struggle with worthiness,

My God-self finished my prayer.

Growing in awareness,

My new Being manifested itself as Love.

Through the doorway, Earth came into view.

All creation shown as Love in its exquisiteness:

Love, the trees; Love, the birds; Love, the grasses;

Love, the snow; Love, the sea; Love, the creatures.

As I circled, swept, and soared, I became Earth.

My heart filled full with such happiness.

To be a part of all this Love —

Joy beyond all Joy!

"This," my Being said, "is Reality."

— Patricia Sheehan (unpublished poem)

Foreword

There is a universal push that is individually and collectively birthing us into a new level of personal and planetary awareness. This transformational urging is pressing in upon us and is forcing us to redefine our priorities. God seems to be saying, "Enough is enough. I have waited for you to come to me in your hearts. I have waited for you to love yourselves enough to heal the suffering of your separation. Very few of you have answered my call. Now I am coming to bring you *home,* and the journey may not be an easy one."

Heart Initiation is about our homecoming. It is about our *assisting* in the transformation, rather than resisting it. The Earth and her evolving inhabitants are moving into a new dimensional frequency. We have gone so far out into our minds and into our left-brained technologies that we have almost lost sight of our higher spiritual natures. We come here to feel and to love, as well as to acquire knowledge and to create. On a deep cellular level, I go into intense anguish if I do not periodically meditate in order to reunite with the true essence of my being. Although I continue to enjoy third-dimensional activities, I must make time for these meditations or I experience deep suffering and an internal longing to reunite with God.

We now have an unprecedented opportunity for becoming free, harmonious, and loving beings, living consciously in a sacred world. If we can see and feel and know what it is we really desire more than anything else in the world, we have a chance of awakening. We must have a vision to make this happen. We must see our alternatives in order to instill a deep desire in our hearts for something more than we have known, something more than the material plane has offered us in our external quest for power, love, and recognition.

The third dimension continues to provide us with an arena for physical manifestation. In part, we come here to create on whatever level we choose. This occupies much of our time, but it has not satisfied our deep longing for spiritual intimacy with the Heart of the True Self, the God within us all. On a feeling level, humanity is bored and restless; it is experiencing an ongoing sense of missing something that is vital to being at peace within one's self. Relationship intimacy has been primarily relegated to sexual interaction and we, as a culture, are starving for love. We are hungry for a sense of being at home within ourselves and of being at peace with our planet and each other.

We know there is much more and we want it, but what we really want is to feel good inside. The anger at being separate has become so intense that part of the world has gone mad. Many people abuse each other without even realizing it. Some people are even killing their fellow human beings in an attempt to stave off their anguish. Each of us faces the challenges of realizing our freedom from the bondage of the separated self; no one is exempt. There is a dying and there is a birthing that connects us all to the hope of a new world consciousness. The path to reunion with God appears to be different for different people, but perhaps there are enough similarities to allow us to speak of the challenges that many of us are experiencing along the way.

It is my hope that this book will give you a personal and planetary vision that will keep you focused on your awakening in a positive way. Your response to the purifying fires of your own transformation may determine the ease with which you enter the next cycle of creation. Our spiritual overseers are giving us tremendous support for moving into the new millennium as free, conscious, and divine human beings. Day by day we are being shown how to live as a united force, born naturally into the wisdom and the power of our Creator through the door of the heart.

Some of you are urgently knocking at this door. You are diligently seeking ways to release all of your egoic guises of control.

Those of you in the throes of transformation are dying to that which has bound you to the past and to all separative belief systems. You are consciously breaking from any attachment you may still have to the illusions of the mass world mind. You are taking responsibility for merging with your soul. The soul is the level of the spiritual Self that is being awakened first and its natural home is in the heart. When the soul is resonating with compassion and real love, it has the capacity to unify your heart with all the many dimensional facets of the Self. I will probably say more than once that the *heart* is the key to Unity or Christ Consciousness.

Heart Initiation is meant to assist you in surrendering as gracefully as possible to that spiritual Self which is wanting to fill your heart, your mind, and your body with the truth of God as Love. Every life on Earth gives you an opportunity to expand into greater and greater levels of this unconditional Love until you totally experience yourself as One with God. Your original birth out of the core of Creation is therein remembered. Within the flame of every heart is the seed of this remembrance. The pure Love that is always hidden within the splendor of this flame can draw on both the wisdom and the power of God.

We have been given the free will to create with our minds as well as to feel with our hearts. The joy of material manifestation can be harmonized with living from that *still, center point* which is always One with God. To maintain that pure *point* of resonance with God while still living within the physical world is what I am calling the *Heart Initiation*.

— Julianne Everett

Part One

CONSCIOUS ASCENSION

The Inevitable Process
of an
Evolving Species

The Christ Process

"Stand fast therefore in the liberty by which Christ has made us free, and do not be entangled again with a yoke of bondage."
— Galatians 5:1

WE ARE EACH BORN with an immense challenge: to spiritually awaken within a sleeping world. We have come to a magical planet whose inhabitants delight in the magnetic allure of their physical manifestations. Each day we are faced with coordinating a body, a mind, an emotional nature, and an immortal spiritual Self. We are being called to remember who we are and why we originally came from Source to inhabit this "Garden of Eden" in the universe.

We have incarnated time and again only to get lost in the maze of illusion. The overall fear and suffering on this planet has now brought us to an emotional point of crisis. Humanity is crying out for love; we want to know that God is real and we want to experience Truth and real compassion. Every man, woman, and child can be awakened, enlightened, and God-realized when he or she truly desires — above all else — to live from and *as* the Heart of the One Self.

"Time is measured by cyclic ages, and the gate to every age is a milestone in man's journey toward Light. The touch of Time has opened another age. It will be an age of preparation — preparation for the Kingdom of Immanuel, which is God in man.

"Man now believes that the source of his power lies within the realm of his own strength and cunning because only in that realm can he see and touch. But power from this source is sorely limited, while the power of the Holy Breath reaches beyond the concept of human mind, just as its nature is beyond the sense of touch or sight." [1]

We have been given the gift of God's Spirit within the *Holy Breath*. This Holy Breath is shared by all of life on every level of creation. It is the spiritual life-force that we inhale along with oxygen. We need oxygen in order to physically survive; we need Holy Breath, or *prana*, in order to spiritually survive. Prana is one of our greatest gifts. It is the eternal essence that gives us life by filling our minds, hearts, and bodies with the spirit of creation. Breath allows us to use sound and the spoken word for communicating. It also gives us the co-creative privilege of calling forth the unseen forces of the universe through the power of invocation.

We can pray and expect to be answered. We can ask for God's intercession. We can call forth the archangels, the Ascended Masters and the great Cosmic Beings, as well as that being who came into physical embodiment as Y'shua ben Yosef, more widely known as Jesus. It is within our dominion to serve and to be served by all of those who make up what is called the Spiritual Hierarchy. Lightworkers [2] generally agree that they have come to Earth to serve what they feel is the Divine Plan. None of us really know what that Plan is, but it seems to involve living and working together in greater love and harmony. Dr. Deepak Chopra says that a spiritually awakened person is one who is living in Unity Consciousness. This is the same thing as living in Christ Consciousness, and it exists when you, as the knower, become one with the knowledge; when you, as the observer, become one with what is being observed. When

---

[1] From *Blessed Among Women: The Birth, Life, Ministry, Ascension and Coronation of Mary, Mother of Jesus*, by Arnold Michael.

[2] Those who have dedicated themselves to increasing the Light (Divine Intelligence) and Divine Love on this planet.

sustaining this state of being (also called *Oneness*), one is continually magnetizing and expanding the vibration of love.

As love radiates out into the consciousness of the whole, it naturally heals and brings back into the One all that is living in separation. Free will allows this reunion to take place only according to the desire and mental disposition of the incarnate self. Not everyone wants to become one with God; not everyone even wants to attain Christ Consciousness. Part of the play on this planet is to examine and experience the power of living here as separate beings! The individualized self chooses to experience, and eventually to master, the challenges that exist in both duality and diversity.

When the ego-body-mind has learned the lessons of separation, the soul then begins to call its missing fragments back into wholeness. Since your soul was originally created within a unified field of divine Love, it recognizes and eventually answers the call to reunite with the true Self as Love. My soul's desire at this time is to live here on Earth as this awakened Self, able to use the full potential of the physical body and world, and yet not be bound by the time restrictions of a third-dimensional existence. When one awakens to the soul as the Christ within, one enters into the first stages of Unity Consciousness. The ongoing development of this consciousness is what I am calling the *Christ Process*. It involves awakening within the dream of the illusions that have kept us believing that we are separate, solid beings living temporarily on a third-dimensional planet.

Jesus came, as do all true teachers and avatars, to assist in lifting the consciousness of the planet into greater levels of compassion, loving service, and wisdom. He came to dispel fear and the myth of separation. He taught us how to love and how to live in Oneness with God. It is my understanding and my personal experience that Jesus, known to some of you as Sananda, is still with us. In fact, he has proven to me beyond a shadow of a doubt that no one ever really *leaves*. As energy, vibration, and consciousness, ALL non-physical beings live on indefinitely. They learn and serve on any plane or dimension of being that will continue to support their desires and their ongoing spiritual development. New bodies of love, light, and intelligence are created according to the requirements of the services being rendered, and according to the consciousness of the one who has transitioned.

The Christ Jesus and beloved Mary initiated me into the spiritual worlds. They awakened me in the 1960s by showing me the energy matrices that make up the etheric substance around, through, and within the Earth. The first dimensional matrix is commonly called the *astral* or *psychic plane* and it contains the thoughts and feelings of humanity. Our disharmonious, confusing, and fear-based thoughts have created a heavy spectrum of consciousness that has kept us feeling separate from the rest of creation. Part of my initiation was to be able to penetrate and pass through the illusions of the astral plane so that I could be introduced to the next stratum of consciousness, called the *akashic plane*. This is where the living records of creation are stored. The akashic is lighter than the astral plane in feeling and it appears to be more holographic in character. I suppose that the substance of the astral plane is also holographic, but it is so much heavier that it feels almost physical. The akasha contains the ongoing living records of individuals, families, groups, planets, galaxies, and universes.

Beloved Jesus and Mary came day after day to stabilize me within these new worlds. Before they introduced me to the astral and akashic planes, I knew nothing about other planes or dimensions of being. The experiences they took me through within these first non-physical realms of creation were totally unexpected. I was also shown that Christ *lives* as a conscious energy field inside of my heart and that this resonating field of loving intelligence is always one with my soul. I have since been told that my own I AM Presence called Mary and Jesus forth to birth and awaken the Christ Flame within my spiritual heart. Evidently, it was my time to lift the first veils of illusion. These experiences were the beginning of my true spiritual training.

Later I discovered that the desire to consciously reunite with the Christ actually came from the longing of my lower self, which wanted to terminate my suffering. Now, thirty years later, I am finding that the pangs of separation that I felt so deeply in my twenties, stemmed not only from my desire to reunite with God, but also from my desire to reconnect with my own soul through the opening of my heart! One can realize material success, sexual joy, a beautiful physical body, a great relationship, and an outwardly fulfilling lifestyle and still find no real peace within. Until the soul is awakened within the heart as love, the void tugs and the emptiness remains.

Jesus, as the ascended Christ, is answering the call of many souls as he oversees the final years of his 2,000-year dispensation. A dispensation is a period of time given to an avatar for bringing the minds and hearts of humanity into a more expanded level of Unity Consciousness. Jesus, or Y'shua ben Josef, seems to be making sure that the *true* message of the Christ is delivered and understood during these final few years of his dispensation. The word "Christ" comes from the Greek word *Cristos*, meaning the *anointed one*. Heart Initiation refers to receiving an anointing of the heart which has the potential to awaken one into a more loving and compassionate state of being.

Past, present, and future avatars are working together in Unity Consciousness to help us remember our Oneness. There they live and serve as one body of living, loving intelligence, as do all the members of the Spiritual Hierarchy, both on and off planet. Whenever we are working within these collective forcefields of divine Love, Wisdom, and Power, then we are working with and as a *group avatar* for the evolutionary development of this planet. Love is the most powerful force in the universe, and it is the key to Unity or Christ Consciousness. Love does not, however, always fit our pictures and ideals *about* love. When we learn to recognize and feel the essence of true love as it comes to us and through us, then we have a chance of embodying our divinity.

Appearances in this world would lead us to believe that there are good and bad people, that there are right and wrong ways of doing things, and that some people are spiritually more advanced than others. If we really want to experience Oneness — with God and with each other — then we cannot separate out the so-called "righteous ones." If we engage in the practice of *judging others,* we contribute to and perpetuate the experience of separation from God and from each other. Some of you have incarnated this time in order to practice living in compassion, and to see if you can bring new levels of unconditional love into your lives and the lives of others. We, as a culture, have not given due recognition to our spiritual nature. Now we are each being reminded of our highest and deepest desires. To actualize ourselves as divine human beings is no easy task, and yet the time has come for many of us to do so.

The beloved Christ Jesus and Mother Mary eventually initiated me into increasingly higher levels of the Self. I got to experience angels and masters who live in continuous joy and love. I was introduced to, and proceeded to be educated by, those who are known as the *Ascended Masters*. It is my challenge to sustain the peaceful and loving radiations that these beings continue to initiate into my consciousness when I am with them on the higher dimensions. These experiences are not always retained by my conscious mind. They remain, however, an integral part of the memory fields that surround and penetrate my being, and the information that I need from these inner-plane experiences seems to come forth as necessary. Defining these expanded levels of consciousness, and assisting people in developing interdimensional relationships is now a part of my service here on Earth. The gift has been given; I simply have chosen to share it as best I can.

Once you focus your intent on living from the heart, then your own individualized Christ Process will continually refine and redefine what you need to do to stay awake at the soul (or heart) level of the Self. When you learn to listen and heed the voice of your heart, then you will experience merging with your soul. The next step is to consciously merge with your *I AM Presence,*[3] or what is sometimes referred to as your *oversoul*. This facet of the Self is energetically connected to many other dimensions of your being. We each seem to be programmed, or spiritually encoded, to awaken in time to prepare our minds and bodies to take in ever higher spectrums of love, light, and intelligence.

Even after the soul is awakened, it is often difficult to sustain Unity Consciousness. The ways of the Earth are powerfully seductive and familiar. We have been living in duality consciousness for a long, long time. The ego often likes to remain safe, comfortable, and unchallenged. It is up to you to choose whether or not you want to live on the edge, or beyond. And then again, your soul may awaken you whether you *think* you are prepared or not!

One of the reasons we have resisted being fully conscious and alive on this planet is that we have been so afraid of pain and suffering. We know that if we awaken, we will *feel* more! Astral energies are constantly stimulating our personalized and collective memory fields through our nervous system. These fields keep giving us pictures that are founded in the fear and the pain of the past. The movies that are in our theaters often amplify these pictures, filling our lower emotional bodies with such fear that the astral plane gains increasing power over our connection to our soul. The astral dimension is like a huge mirror, reflecting pictures from both above and below. I will devote a later chapter to exploring its function in our lives.

The ego-body-mind is programmed to survive. It thinks and feels that it has to use its memory in order for you to survive in a conditional, third-dimensional world. There is memory, however, beyond the third dimension, and it is these higher memory fields that are now being contacted and made available to the conscious mind. When true joy is radiating and emanating from an incarnate being, that joy is coming from the heart of a soul that is in

---

3   The I AM or God Presence is the most transcendent facet of the individualized soul. This aspect of the Self sustains one's highest consciousness by holding a radiant field of God's Love and Light around the body. The Presence does not come completely into the body since It lives in the seventh dimension. As we lift into higher and higher dimensions, more of the Presence can come into the body.

attunement with God. Joy exists as a normal state of being on the higher dimensions. When we live and breathe *beyond* the astral plane and the memory fields of the akasha, then we can live here as liberated souls. The ego-body mind is only a small part of your total existence, and it is the only part of you that is bound to the pain of the past!

Most of us are highly creative when it comes to ways in which we can keep ourselves from feeling the suffering that has been recorded within the cellular and astral spectrums of the self. What we usually do not know is that power often resides in tandem with the fear to express it, just as joy lives in the wake of sadness, and compassion is on the other side of suffering.

TO FEEL EVERYTHING WITHIN THE SELF,

AND EVERYONE AS THE SELF,

IS TO BE FULLY ALIVE!

Humankind has not yet decided if it wants to be that awake or that alive. However, there are a considerable number of incarnate beings who are growing tired of trying to find happiness in the outer world. Many people are finding that they are no longer able to satisfy their deeper spiritual needs through external satisfactions. The usual third-dimensional activities that used to bring pleasure are now amplifying the emptiness they feel inside, causing depression, fear, and confusion. This is a promising step towards real transformation, because those who are discontent will hopefully start looking within to find the true *home* of the soul and its purpose here on Earth.

In Latin the word for person is *persona*, and it means "mask" or "character in a play." Sometimes we get so involved in the character we have developed for expressing ourselves here on Earth that we forget who we truly are. In order to survive, we have become adept at using our persona for hiding the thoughts and feelings that we do not want others to see. If the ego is insecure, it also uses the persona to stay in control and *on top* of others. After you align with your Higher Self [4] and function more from that part of your being, you will begin to recognize whether you are acting out of "survival" or out of love. You will notice if and when your ego is trying to keep you from looking weak or disempowered. If you really want to transform negative patterning, then the mask must be removed.

FIRST YOU MUST KNOW AND

THEN REALLY ACCEPT THAT

"REVEALING IS HEALING"...

Otherwise, you will not want to go through the disclosure part of the Christ Process, or to let go of the programming that your personality may have adopted in order for you to feel safe. Most of us are just touching on what it means to live, love, and communicate from Unity Consciousness. We have been living in spiritual isolation for many thousands of years under the misguided notion that we were free and awake, when in truth we have been confined by our thoughts and our relationship to time. On the positive side, these years of separation have made us mentally and physically strong and capable. On the negative side, they have filled us with fear and massive delusions about life, relationships, and authentic love and power.

During some of the workshops and conferences I have attended and facilitated over the last thirty years, I have occasionally been part of a group anointing. What emerges during these special moments, hours, and sometimes days is beyond everyone's fondest dreams. Divine Love, most probably from Divine Beings, seems to use these gatherings for reaching in and opening hearts. The facilitators do make a difference, since they direct the energies to keep them moving deeper and deeper into the hearts of the participants.

---

[4] The Higher Self denotes that part of the Self that is living in Unity or Christ Consciousness.

At first just a few people appear to be touched. Eventually, love expands to embrace the whole group like a giant wave; in its wake is palpable transformation. These group anointings cause all kinds of reactions in people — from pain to ecstasy — as old and new feelings are revealed. Everyone that speaks is felt, and those who hold back are also felt. There is much crying, much laughing, and much physical and spiritual touching.

These wondrous experiences are sometimes difficult to sustain after one leaves the group matrix. Participants know that they have received a rare gift, and they want to share it with everyone. Some go on to join other groups in the hopes that they will also be opened at the heart. Every opportunity that we have to see, feel, and touch the Oneness is a blessed event. Whether these anointings are experienced by an individual or a group, they always give one a true feeling of wholeness. It is wonderful to see and feel beyond the words.

If we were to remain in ecstasy without it being founded in the whole of the Self, we would not realize our mastery here on Earth. Many metaphysical people are adept at going out of their bodies in order to have spiritual experiences. This kind of exploration can be useful to one's overall development, but it usually expands the mind more than it does the heart. The heart chakra is the central connector for getting our bodies into Christ Consciousness. We have many other spiritual energy centers,[5] and they must all be unified with the heart in order to make a whole-body shift into the fourth and fifth dimensions. Our spiritual energy centers, or chakras, connect our physical and subtle bodies. The subtle bodies are multidimensional systems of intelligence, often called *Lightbodies*. These bodies are fascinating to explore, but first things first.

It is too bad that transformation involves purification, but it seems to be a necessary component of lasting change. That is why crucifixion and resurrection are both a part of the Christ Process.

---

[5] These centers are also called *chakras*, which is a Hindi word meaning *spinning wheels*. These chakras act as computers for the body.

There must be a release, a letting go of the old, a dying to what is no longer needed before a resurrection can actually take place. The Christ Process refers to an ever-expanding journey that is progressively leading one into full Unity Consciousness.

In the Hindu religion, God is described as having three major facets known as Brahma, Vishnu, and Shiva: the Creator, the Preserver, and the Destroyer. As you will discover later on in this book, Shiva, the destroyer aspect of God, has become one of my greatest initiators. I can tell you that I never expected to see Shiva in this or any other lifetime! I have since been shown that he is very much a part of directing the purifying forces into the third-dimensional world during this time in our collective spiritual development. He is a part of preparing the people of this planet for accelerated transformation. I really like to think of Shiva as the dissolution aspect of God, rather than as the destroyer. He comes forth to assist us in letting go of what is no longer serving the Divine Mother, who is now very present in our world. She is here to birth and to resurrect the old energies into the new. She works through a collective body of conscious beings known as the Cosmic World Mother, and they are a major force of transformation on our planet at this time. They are releasing the Grace of Mother God that we need to ascend into Christ Consciousness. They represent the love, the wisdom, and the power of the divine feminine, which is being called forth within us all in order to balance the patriarchal energies that have held sway for so long.

The pain and suffering in your world appears to be real. It feels sometimes like a permanent condition that will always exist on your planet. You, as a race of third-dimensional beings, have dreaded going in and looking beneath the sorrow of your separation, but therein lies the gift for which you have been searching. We have come to assist you in releasing the agony of your past, and to help you to let go and transmute the pictures that have continued to have you believe that your separation is real and permanent.

The joy of transcendence is riding quickly on your heels if you can untie the cords that continue to bind you to the choices you made so long ago. We bring you the gift of Divine Grace. We have come to birth you into the pure bliss of your heart, for therein lies your soul's remembrance. God resides as a permanent dweller in the temple of your heart. It is the desire for reunion with this God-Presence within your own heart which has kept your feet on the path during your outgoing cycle of darkness.

Trust your process to take you ever deeper and ever higher; trust your soul to bring you into the depths of your being; trust your I AM Presence to bring you into the heights of your being; and trust your spirit, which was created out of pure love, to prepare your body for its full transfiguration into a body of living Light.

— The divine feminine through the
collective intelligence of the Cosmic World Mother

You may *think* that you do not have any pain to release or heal. I have found that deep suffering exists within the collective memory of all humans. When abiding in the body, pain is felt intensely as one's own; when abiding in the Higher Self, pain will still be felt but it can be observed from a different perspective. Pain alerts us that something is out of order, and that *something* wants to be heard. The physical and emotional bodies are very connected. Emotional suffering eventually works its way into the body, where it tries to communicate by using pain as its language. Doctors are now coming forth to publicly declare that women who have breast cancer, for example, are not getting enough love or support.

Sometimes feelings become so powerful that they can physically break down the energy systems that keep the heart in working order. Heart attacks are just one example of how much people need and want to be loved. When it comes to a stroke, then these misaligned energies have found their way to the head, where intense pressure causes the blood vessels to rupture in the brain. Emotional, mental, and physical diseases eventually become genetic, and they are carried within the family tree until someone breaks the chain of suffering and separation. Disease and disharmony on every level would be far less prevalent in this world if we would stop blaming others and shaming ourselves. We need to make healing ourselves and our relationships a priority if we want to release the root causes of our planetary anguish.

We need to break down the walls of our suffering if we really want to bring our hearts into the deep love and compassion that we so desperately crave for ourselves and our world. *This is a very heightened and sacred moment in our planetary history*. Our spiritual overseers are asking us to purify ourselves so that we can embody our forgotten divinity. We are receiving a tremendous influx of spiritual energy so that we can make a personal and a planetary shift in consciousness. This energy intensification is penetrating all of life, and it is making some people feel even more afraid and desperate. It is unleashing the pain that most of us have been trained to repress. Since early childhood we are often told to *control* our feelings. For the most part, the feminine or feeling aspect of humanity has been held in denial. This has taken its toll on our emotional well-being.

Our feelings are the key to the door of the heart, and the heart is what connects us to our Source. Love precedes both authentic power and true wisdom. Lasting freedom can only come through merging with the love and the truth that is the natural state of an opened heart. All that you have accomplished has shed light on the many facets of your being. Your spirit is always leading you down the path of the heart, preparing your mind and your body to receive the fullness of the Christ.

Very few people in all of history have ever embodied the truth or the ordeal of becoming a Christ. True compassion embraces and transcends suffering in others. The ordeal is in the development of compassion through one's own suffering. Enter into the image of the self – the hologram of your persona – until the pain of separation is felt within every cell. Enter into such union with others that you can know of their separation as well. That is the depth of intimacy that it takes to create the miracles that heal and lift the whole; that is the kind of union that is the key to shaking off the ignorance and illusions that have kept us in separation. The willingness to feel every living expression of God within oneself is the hallmark of true compassion. Those who are willing to face the challenges of their own personal transformation and to awaken to the Christ within their own hearts are the ones who are going to have the strength, the compassion, and the power to shift the mass consciousness from death to life and from fear to love. They are the ones who are preparing for the Holy Spirit to completely consume the body.

The Anointing

"But as it is written: 'Eye has not seen, nor ear heard, nor have entered into the heart of man the things which God has prepared for those who love Him.'"

— I Corinthians 2:9

THERE IS A MYSTICAL ANOINTING that takes place within the hearts of all sincere seekers which involves being spiritually *touched* by the Holy Spirit. This anointing seems to *quicken* the flow of Light and Love within the hearts, the minds, *and* the bodies of all those who have been touched. Many of you have experienced being anointed with water through baptism, generally performed very early in life. This sacred and beautiful commitment to God through the medium of holy water is often our first introduction to the Christ concept. Some experience another kind of baptism by what might be called *Holy Light*.

My first and primary anointing by Light occurred when I was in my twenties. It all started in an early morning dream. In the dream, a large ball of intensely brilliant golden-white light appeared as a blazing sun rising over the crest of a mountain. The light of this sun became so bright that I finally had to end the dream by opening my eyes. I was totally overwhelmed when I saw that this "sun" was in my bedroom! It was about four feet in diameter, and it hovered and glowed in a brilliant radiance that was almost blinding.

This ball of radiant light started moving towards me, and then it began to enter my body. I watched my arms slowly begin to dissolve into Light, and I remember *shouting* to myself " ... I'm becoming the Light. I am the Light, I am the Light — and everything in and around me is *only* this Light ... everything!" I knew that this had to be true because I was watching my arms and then my whole body slowly turning into this amazingly loving light. As I continued to merge with this "sun" and to watch my physical body dissolve, I felt like I was everything in the universe, and yet I was nothing but this simple, pure ball of light. It was a great and humbling realization.

The merging became so intense that I began to feel as though I was making love with a cosmic ball of light! This union created a kind of cellular release that lasted for about six hours. Although I have spiritually encountered this ball of light several times since this initial experience, it has never consumed my physical substance in exactly the same way. This first experience was my primary anointing by God's Light.

In retrospect, I now believe that this ball of light was probably the manifestation of my own God-Presence, and that it came to awaken the Christ within my heart. Merging with the Light that day released so much spiritual remembrance within my being that the seed of the Christ Flame within my heart awakened. When this happens, there is no turning back. The initiatic process of the Christ had truly begun.

The Christ-self bridges our visible human expression with our generally invisible I AM Presence, which is our highest and least dense body. The Presence sustains the Holy Spirit's perfection within a Diamond Lightbody, that surrounds and penetrates the physical vehicleThe Anointing so that we have a template for remembering the Immortal Self. This beloved Presence remains forever untainted by the thoughts or feelings of the incarnated self. It acts, therefore, as a constant reminder of our Source. Some see the I AM Presence as no more than a mere spark of Light. It is, nonetheless, a living intelligence, capable of manifesting a form in any dimension that is appropriate to the service being rendered.

THE "I AM PRESENCE" IS THE ORIGINAL EMANATION OF THE SELF AS A FORMED UNIT OF CONSCIOUSNESS FROM OUT OF THE HEART AND MIND OF GOD.

The anointing by Light is often given to a Heart Initiate at a special time of readiness. It occurs because one's soul has sent forth its call to earnestly begin the Christ Process. The Lord Jesus promised his disciples that they would be receiving the indwelling of the Holy Spirit after his ascension. Their dramatic anointing is biblically referred to as Pentecost. It occurred seven weeks after Jesus' resurrection. I believe that Jesus the Christ also promised this to all future generations, and that most of us in some life or another have prayed to God to receive the fullness of the Holy Spirit. It is very possible that an anointing takes place in every life where one has consciously chosen to focus on living the true principles of the Christ within his or her heart.

The anointing awakens the Initiate because it quickens the Light within the cellular body and releases some of the pure memory of who we are and why we are here, in the true spiritual sense. When an anointing takes place, it ignites the heart's earnest passion to reunite with God. It sets into action an Initiate's desire to be released from the limitations of the human condition. It creates an impulse within the heart which can never be forgotten. It also awakens the etheric body, which is the first layer of subtle energy surrounding the physical self. The dimensional layers of Light and Love which envelop us are often referred to as separate *bodies,* because they each exist as a form within the frequency wave band to which they are attuned.

The anointing can bring forth the awareness of oneself within his or her emotional body, which is often attuned to the astral octaves within the lower fourth dimension. That dimension is often difficult for us to deal with because it contains a mixture of illumined truth and the partial truth that is born from humanly misqualified[6] thoughts and feelings. The fourth dimension houses the psychic fields of delusion that often distract even the most sincere seekers. It is imperative that the Heart Initiate does not get sidetracked by fascination with the astral plane. It is very alluring because emotional substance is magnetic and has a literal pull on the vibrational octaves of the self that may still be wanting to act out the desires of the lower human ego.

To get in touch with your "hidden" fantasies or desires, watch what kind of activities you are attracted to in your dreams. The astral plane is the easiest to access because it is the closest to the physical. It is often the first and only plane that psychics can access. Here they can sometimes read auras[7] and the lower octaves of the Akashic records.[8] It is tempting for one who is psychically open to relay this astral *sensing* to friends or clients as though it were the ultimate truth. When sharing information that you may be receiving from the thought projections within another's aura, it must be presented as your own perception, and nothing more. In that way you will not accrue any new karma.[9]

Every sincere seeker who wishes to live more consciously and permanently in the dimensions that are beyond duality, must at some time face the astral challenges that are within the lower octaves of

---

6   Thoughts and feelings that have not been created by the unlimited Christ-self but rather by one's mental and emotional conditioning.

7   The subtle energy fields which surround the physical body. The aura contains a person's mental and emotional thought projections.

8   Living records which are transcribed upon the ethers according to the dimension in which the action took place.

9   Used here in reference to the Law of Cause and Effect: "As one reaps, he sows." In Hinduism and Buddhism, karma determines one's destiny in his or her next existence.

10 The hidden or dark side of one's nature naturally polarizes with one's light side until Unity Consciousness is understood and lived.

11 Refers to our capacity to embrace and release the separative belief systems that have bound us into limited thinking and feeling.

the fourth dimension. When the separative beliefs and illusions of the shadow self [10] are understood and loved free,[11] then there is more room for integrating the Higher Self and more room for the essence of the Holy Spirit to fill the body.

It is the intensity of an Initiate's desire, coupled with the divine blueprint of their I AM Presence, that determines the time it takes for him or her to move through each stage of the Christ Process. To transform and resurrect one's lower nature, one must let go of all parts of the self that are in limitation and separation. When the individualized soul becomes aware of itself as love, then the Christ-self (as the transformational energy of love) can begin resurrecting the physical, mental, emotional, and etheric bodies into increasingly refined frequencies of living light.

What we eventually long for, above all else, is to live in union with God at all times — *especially* while we are living and serving in the density of a third-dimensional world! The primal root of our innate suffering comes from thinking and feeling that we are separate from our Source. These thoughts and feelings have created belief systems that are no longer serving our evolution. While incarnational patterns vary, most of us who have had many lives on Earth have done it all. Spiritual aspiration was part of some lives and not others. The chief aim of incarnation is to enable Spirit/ God to experience everything! We have raped, we have been raped; we have killed, we have been killed; and on and on.

The desire to ascend is high in this lifetime because this is the lifetime in which many will ascend! The urgings of our Spirit are always in alignment with our life's purpose; our Spirit is always in alignment with our Divine Plan — after all, It created the Plan!

The Crucifixion

"We are all naive to the requirements of awakening ... it comes down to being crucified innumerable times. Although youth likes to make efforts to awaken through the body, higher centers awaken through transforming emotional suffering."
— *Self Remembering*, by Robert Burton

THE POLARIZED FORCEFIELDS WHICH HOLD US IN FORM and the glandular secretions which keep us healthy and vital both shut down temporarily when our bodies contract in fear. Most of us automatically stop breathing for short periods of time when we experience physical, mental, or emotional trauma. No matter how insignificant they may appear to be at the time, these traumas add up. We die a little on a cellular level every time we cut off our life force. We also die a little every time we avoid the emotional challenge of being fully present, fully honest, and fully alive.

The body always seems to respond in direct relationship to the state of one's mind and emotions. The natural rhythm of my breathing gets totally disrupted if I think too much about the past or the future. My breath also shortens if I talk too much or forget where I am. For example, if I am alone in the car and mentally start planning a workshop for next weekend, my mind quickly disassociates from the body, my breath shortens or momentarily stops, and sometimes I actually forget where I am! Anytime I leave the present moment through time-bound thinking or speaking, my body *thinks* that I am afraid, and it responds by stopping the flow of my life force. Although we think of breathing as an autonomous biological process, it is directly linked with thinking, speaking, and feeling.

Fear is a survival response brought forth by the ego-body-mind in its attempt to remain safe. When the individualized ego is faced with unfamiliar territory on any plane or dimension of being, the ego reacts with fear — the fear of death. The will to live has actually become polarized with the fear of dying because we have not cellularly accepted our spiritual immortality. Passing from the spirit world into a physical world at birth and passing back again into the spirit world at death have been two of our most powerful and most difficult transitions. The emotional, mental, and physical bodies have not generally been programmed to let go of the familiar or to face the unfamiliar with faith and ease of passage. What we are preparing to do during this cycle of our evolution has not been done before except by a rare few. Although we use interdimensional bodies between physical incarnations, we have not been passing from one body to the next without going through the transition called *death*.

Crucifixion is not about death as we have known it. It is about letting go and moving into new territory with faith, power, love, and wisdom. We are all in this together as true spiritual pioneers. To let go of our fear of death, we must each seek out why we have pain and fear associated with just being ourselves in every moment. How can we more honestly express our true thoughts and feelings, especially in the moments that we are experiencing fear and feeling separate? Taking off the mask of the ego's persona and letting go of the desire to look good or appear powerful at all costs is the challenge that all sentient beings must face if they choose to awaken into the freedom of their own Christ Consciousness.

THE CRUCIFIXION DEMANDS THAT THE HUMAN SELF BE BROUGHT OUT OF DENIAL AND INTO TRUTH.

To live in truth, one must be willing to look at every thought, feeling, and action with exquisite integrity, personally and impersonally evaluating their content in relationship to awakening. One must be willing to die to that which is no longer serving the I AM Presence and to transcend the mental and emotional patterning that has *not* been trained to stay focused at the heart. It takes a tremendous act of faith to surrender to the Christ as the consciousness of unconditional love within the heart, and perhaps it takes even more faith to actively live from the wisdom of that love. The meaning of unconditional love is often misunderstood and I am, therefore, being guided to share with you the following transmission from the beloved Mother Mary:

Conditional love only exists in conditional worlds. Unconditional love only exists in unconditional worlds. Perhaps this alone defines the kind of love that is needed to sustain the many worlds that continue to support your journey into divinity. You have found it important to experience the limitations of earthly love; perhaps now you will find it equally important to taste the nectar of unlimited love. If you find yourself or others unlovable, then the bitterness returns, but the nectar is always within the bitterness, so do not despair.

To free ourselves from ages of self-imposed bondage and the reactive natures that we have developed in response to that bondage, we need to see life and everyone in it from a much more cosmic perspective. This higher viewpoint must not only be anchored in the unconditional love of an opened heart, but it must also be based on a power that is founded on wisdom and discernment. Love — especially unconditional love — must be balanced with wisdom in order to keep us from leaning too far into the intuitive faculties of the right hemisphere of our brain. The right hemisphere sources our creativity, but as far as I know we are not able to manifest its talents without incorporating the linear processes of the left hemisphere.

The "flower children" of the 1960s certainly gave many of us a taste of what can happen when love is not balanced with wisdom. Many people awakened as if from a great sleep. I was living as an ordinary housewife one day and as a crazy *hippie* the next. There was no logical reason for this incredible shift in my values, but suddenly I became totally childlike and unconditionally loving. There were times when I thought that I was really going to go completely insane. My family would be the first to tell you that I was no longer of this world. I was living on different dimensions simultaneously, and without drugs!

Thank God most of my own family had a spiritual or a metaphysical background! My hippie buddies during that time were all managing to get themselves awakened one way or another. Close friendships developed which will never be forgotten. There was a sense of having been thrown together from all different walks of life to do some kind of service that none of us really understood. We just knew that we wanted to open up as fast as we could, to feel more love, and to have a glimpse into other realities.

The 1960s provided a very fertile ground for awakening the heart and the creative right brain of many people who were destined to be a part of changing the consciousness of humanity. The '60s jolted the mass consciousness out of its complacency, and I think that those years will go down in history as the true beginning of this century's spiritual revolution. The "flower children" gave humankind a very important facet to the diamond mirror of our greater collective Self.

The Crucifixion brings us into a maturing cycle. It is now time for many of us to bring our gifts into the world. Spiritually speaking, the 1960s children are now in their "thirties." It is time for exercising true wisdom and for practicing discernment, time to serve as Initiates of the Heart, and time to support the spiritual advancement of the Divine human. To surrender into Crucifixion, we need to trust God through our own I AM Presence, and we need to trust our relationship to the Divine Plan. What does this really mean? I called forth the Presence of the Ascended Master Jesus/Sananda, and received the following transmission:

In the time that I lived as Jesus, it was important to stress the unification between man and God as one intelligent whole being of consciousness. The Christ that you speak of is a state of being, or a state of living in the Oneness with Light and Love as the absolute sustaining force of all creation. The Creator's Plan, or the Divine Plan, is simply the constant expanding of this Love and Light. Your spiritual relationship to the expanding forces of creation will keep unfolding, revealing to you your part in sustaining the forces of life everlasting. It is impossible to destroy these forces, but appearances would sometimes have you believe that death is a part of life.

The seed frequency of the Christ — as "Divine Love," as "Unity Consciousness," or as "living in Oneness with God" — is within every heart. The all-out commitment to awaken the consciousness of the Christ within is a major component of the ascension process. We have the potential for ascending in this lifetime: the ingredients are there. In fact, the cake is already in the oven! Part of being able to resonate and live within the Christ frequency is determined by your willingness to witness your thoughts, feelings, and actions. This is not about engendering more guilt; it is about increasing self-awareness without judgment.

With your intention and desire, the I AM Presence will keep expanding the love, the wisdom and the power within your heart. Every day this increase in the Christ vibration will assist you in developing and sustaining Unity Consciousness. As the crucifixion aspect of the Christ Process continues, one becomes increasingly lighter (or sometimes heavier, depending on the spiritual release work that is occurring within the subtle and physical bodies). The Christ Process is, after all, an ongoing refining activity, and we must have the faith that what is happening within us and around us is always in accordance with the Divine Will for our lifestream.

We are living miracles in form. I have no doubt that there is a God, or a conscious power, whose pure Wisdom and Love is constantly creating all of life everywhere. Holographic models suggest that our physical reality is refreshed or re-created many times each second. We assist in this creative process by endlessly retrieving ourselves within the power of the present moment. Only in this precious, eternal now can we really be responsible for our internal and external environments. The advancing Initiate must often utilize their God-given will to stay awake in the garden. Going to sleep is the common reaction of one who does not want to experience fear or feel the pain that the situation is providing as a learning tool.

Wake and pray that you may not enter into temptation; the spirit indeed is willing and ready, but the body is weak.

— Mark 14:38
(*Holy Bible,* Lamsa translation)

At some time or another, every Initiate must face the duality play within the self. According to Robert Johnson, author of *Owning Your Own Shadow,* all that we project into the world has a counterpart, or an opposite polarity. We can get to know this part by watching our attachments. If one is attached to being in the Light, for example, then he or she may be equally opposed to acknowledging their dark side. That opposition creates a *shadow self.* According to Johnson, the aversion to the hidden aspects of ones self only empowers them, and actually attracts them into our experience. How can we deal with this? By acknowledging and becoming the whole *enchilada!* Allowing the so-called negative and positive sides of the self to co-exist is one of the major keys to Unity Consciousness.

We are often so emotionally scarred that we do not want to take a look at our deeper wounds or our darker side. Many lifetimes of trauma and abuse, both given and received, are within our individual and collective memories. Eventually these *wounds* come to abide within our physical bodies, taking up residence where there are already physical or emotional weaknesses due to ancestral or past life patterning. The body also perfectly mirrors or reflects the weaknesses or strengths that you may be transmuting or carrying forward for an entire tribe! An example of this would be the sensitivity that the indigenous tribes have to alchohol. Weak spots in the body act as our teachers. Even though they can eventually create dis-ease and are often associated with tears or holes in the aura (leaving one open to psychic attack and vulnerable to continual abuse by others), they are there to help us focus our attention on mastering the physical and astral dimensions of the self.

We magnetize people and situations to us that will allow us to see where we may need healing. We are constantly acting as mirrors for ourselves and each other. These *mirrors* become clearer as we become more honest and more willing to live in truth. If we are unwilling to face all parts of the self, then we are unwilling to face the Crucifixion part of our Christ Process. Protecting the ego leaves one in a survival mode, and indicates that — at that point in time — the egoic defense structures are stronger than the desire to surrender to God.

The lower emotional or astral body enjoys having its senses stimulated. It is magnetized to excitement and all forms of human drama. The wounded ego likes company and is attracted to others of like consciousness. The healthy ego can play in any field of consciousness and yet know that it does not need to be stimulated to feel good, nor to be in like company to feel whole. If we can align the ego with the Christ-self, then we can bring the emotional, mental, physical, and etheric bodies into the higher dimensions. As we ascend, each of these bodies is being lifted or expanded into whole new frequency wave bands. The functions of our four lower bodies are going to be redefined in relationship to our more refined spiritual senses.

As the lower bodies awaken, the chakras that connect the subtle and physical bodies will begin aligning us with octaves of thinking and feeling not usually experienced by the mind, heart, and body of a physically incarnate being — at least not in our recent history! As we live more and more in the consciousness of the fourth and fifth dimensions, we are beginning to see and feel other people's thoughts, feelings, and energy patterns. Those who are exploring these new dimensions are learning how to successfully bridge worlds. They often find guides and teachers who can assist and train them in the using the new energies.

You can *love* yourself free from the past and enter the new by loving every condition and every person who has ever served in bringing you into the power of this dynamic moment in your Christ Process. If you find you still have judgments, especially self-judgments, you may place them into the Violet Fire of transmutation and forgiveness. To do this, you may want to ask why certain people and circumstances have come into your life. You may or may not get an immediate answer. Sometimes the Grace of understanding is given in a dream, or after you have already forgiven the one in question. If it fits with your own inner guidance, you may call forth your I AM Presence, the archangels, and the Ascended Masters to assist you in forgiving, and in letting go of all that has gone before.

The Heart Flame cannot receive the fullness of the Christ-self until one releases the energies which may be dormant or stuck within the seven primary chakras. Energy blockages often occur within the first three chakras, which are all centered below the heart. Since the lower chakras work in direct relationship to the upper chakras, they hold some of the key energies that we need for awakening the full potential of the four lower bodies. Several Ascended Masters have informed me that all of our chakras need to be fully operational if we are to ascend into the fifth dimension, which is the first true octave of Christ consciousness. It is also the first dimension above duality and the first field of *reality* where beings live in Unity Consciousness.

As we begin to shift into the higher dimensions, the true place of the ego must be understood. Without the mind, the ego has no will of its own. The ego part of us, however, has led us to believe that we are separate beings, since it experiences itself as being distinct and separate from the others it perceives. In psychoanalytic theory, the ego serves as "the organized conscious mediator between the person and reality."[12] The ego is going to remain with us on any plane or dimension where we live, love, learn, and serve

---

[12] *The New Merriam-Webster Dictionary,* 1989 edition.

as individualized beings. The challenge is not in getting rid of the ego; it is in learning how to use it without getting lost or disassociated from Source. We can use the ego and still *live* in Unity Consciousness; this feels to me to be the best of *all* worlds.

Constantly make the call to Source, to Mother/Father God, to your own I AM Presence, or to whomever would represent the highest octave of truth for you, and then be willing to listen. *The call does compel the answer! The question is, are you willing to respond to what you receive?* Mastery involves a deep willingness to penetrate the depths of your mystery. Greater wisdom and power often reside in the veiled recesses of your being. The most hidden corners of your psyche often contain the life lessons which can bring you your greatest understanding, power, and compassion.

WE MUST PERCEIVE OURSELVES
FROM EVERY ASPECT OF THE SELF
IN ORDER TO LET GO OF OUR DELUSIONS.

If we could embrace all parts of the self, and thereby become a witness to our complete unabridged play in the world, then we would probably be able to see much of our present and past life patterning. It is important, however, not to dwell on our negative patterning. The mind plays a role in understanding what is happening, but that is only one part of the healing. A few years ago it was important to find the wounded parts of the self and to give them a lot of attention and power. Now things are very, very different.

We are now living in a state of Divine Grace. This is true for every man, woman, and child on this planet, regardless of what may *appear* to be otherwise. Grace is being bestowed upon us because the Earth is ascending, and we must move quickly now to catch up with her. Our precious planet is shifting into a new frequency by passing through a band of energy called the Photon Belt. Scientists have known about this Photon Belt and its accompanying manasic radiation for at least thirty-three years. Our solar system orbits around a Central Sun, called Alcyone (the brightest star in the constellation of Pleiades), approximately every 25,860 years. Our present-day sun, moon, and planets must pass through the Photon Belt twice during this cycle of time (that is, once moving toward the north and once moving toward the south). During this complete rotation, there are two periods of darkness and two periods of light. The two periods of darkness last for approximately 10,500 years each, and the two periods of light last for 2,000 years each.

This amazing Belt of intensifying light seems to be stimulating our hearts, minds, and bodies into remembering who we are and why we are here at this amazing cosmic moment in our evolutionary journey. The heartbeat of our planet is literally increasing, as she also is awakening from a deep cycle of rest. When we pass into the central shaft of the Photon Belt, which could take place anytime between 1996 and the year 2012, it is quite probable that the intensity of this light could stimulate Christ consciousness on a massive scale. The Belt is already acting as a kind of John the Baptist, by *announcing* the coming of the Christ within the heart of every man, woman, and child who is transmuting and transforming within the intensity of what is happening and the immensity of what is yet to come.

We would probably not be able to function in the third dimension if we were to truly see all that is being cleared from within and around our bodies and world. If we can just accept that we are living in the time of miracles, then the play of our lives will keep unfolding PERFECTLY. You will know who to see to assist you in releasing and healing. The right people will come into your life at the right time. If and when no one comes to help you on the physical plane, then it might be part of your learning process to call forth assistants from the inner planes.

TRUST YOUR LIFE ENOUGH TO KNOW
THAT YOU ARE GETTING, AND CAN RECEIVE,
EXACTLY WHAT YOU REALLY NEED.

We have so much help at this time, it is sometimes unbelievable. Good practitioners are turning up everywhere. They are here at this time to unveil, unwrap, and miraculously assist us in removing the accumulations of the past. When I feel it is time for a *tune-up*, I first call in my beloved, mighty I AM Presence, my guardian angels, my body elemental,[13] the etheric healing teams, and my Ascended Master sponsors.[14] Most of the healers I go to are very aware of energies, meaning they can see and/or feel interdimensionally. They often notice that I come to a session with a team of helpers. Sometimes they receive direct instructions from my interdimensional assistants. My intention is to do whatever is necessary, but usually I just get out of the way and let the healing proceed. I am now able to feel, and sometimes to see, the miraculous healings that are occurring.

Many patterns and traits are within us before birth. Even very young children can suffer from extreme depression. This condition can become so overwhelming that some parents give their children medication to keep them from committing suicide. This is a sign of our times, an indication of the degree to which the human consciousness has become burdened with the emotional debris of the past. We draw those to us who have similar lessons and vibrational energy fields. It is a gift to have relatives and friends who continue to provide us with the mirrors that we have chosen for healing past life patterning.

The human ego needs to know that it is not going to be deserted when you ascend. Because we are leaving the familiar world, you may sometimes feel as though you are dying. Therefore, your emotional, mental, and physical bodies need to be assured that they are going to be included in your ascension. Each of these bodies lives within a specific frequency, or dimension of consciousness, and each body is equally important. If you will just take a few

---

[13] A guardian deva from the elemental kingdom who has agreed since your first incarnation to oversee the intelligence of your physical body.

[14] Ascended Master sponsors are those who have especially elected to oversee the spiritual development of incarnate beings.

moments a day to literally breathe the Love and Light of your I AM Presence into your abdomen, then your lower bodies will surrender more easily to your ongoing Christ Process.

For many thousands of years, the ego (as the individualized focus of awareness) has been centered in the solar plexus chakra, which is the locus of one's personal will. As you ascend, your ego is being called to merge with your soul at the heart (or Christ) level of your Self, thereby eliminating any conflict that may exist between human will and Divine Will. The I AM Presence is quickening the Christ vibration within one's heart by stimulating a fifth-dimensional matrix of intelligence and love, which is both around and within the body. This fifth-dimensional matrix is presently the *home*[15] frequency for the heart chakra. When you awaken within this matrix of the Self you have entered the first true level of your ascension.

Your I AM Presence has its spiritual center in the *Holy of Holies*, which is a vortex within the center of your skull. The Holy of Holies is created through the blending and balancing of three sacred energy fields: the crown chakra at the top of the head, which is related to your pineal gland; the brow chakra in the center of your forehead, which is related to your pituitary gland; and the eighth chakra, sometimes called the *ascension chakra*, which is related to your hypothalamus gland.

According to the I AM teachings,[16] we have a three-fold heart flame. The first flame (on the left side of the heart) is blue, representing Divine Will; the second flame (on the right side of the heart) is pink, representing Divine Love; and the third flame (in the center of the heart) is yellow, representing Divine Wisdom. I have

---

[15] Refers to matching a dimension with the aspect of the self that naturally lives in that frequency.

[16] Refers to a collective body of information given by members of the Spiritual Hierarchy to Godfré Ray and Lotus King. This information was recorded and placed into a series of books published by the Saint Germain Press. The first three books of this series are entitled *The Magic Presence, Original Unveiled Mysteries,* and *The "I AM" Discourses*.

been directed by the Ascended Master Kuthumi to add an amendment to this teaching:

The yellow flame sustains the balanced energies of the masculine and the feminine aspects of the self within the three-fold flame of both the heart and the head. The Holy of Holies, wherein abides the three-fold head Flame, was not a part of the I AM Teachings at the time that they were brought forth in the 1930s. The head flame is encoded to sustain the frequencies of the I AM Presence, and the heart flame is encoded to anchor the frequencies of the Christ. The sacred relationship that vibrationally exists between these two three-fold flames is what allows the heart, the head, and the body to operate as a multidimensional unit of consciousness.

The blue flame within the heart receives and sustains the Father aspect of Divinity and is related to the pineal gland. The pink flame receives and sustains the Mother aspect of Divinity and is related to the pituitary gland, where it stimulates one's ability to see, hear, and feel interdimensionally. The yellow flame receives and sustains the Divine Androgyny aspect of Divinity and is related to the hypothalamus gland.

If your intention is to consciously merge with your I AM Presence, then it will take you through the various stages of initiation that eventually lead to your ascension. Your ego needs to know whether or not you intend to take your body with you when you ascend. These choices will determine your path. If you do decide you want to merge with your soul at the heart level of the self, then the Christ energy (as the vibration of Oneness) will continue to quicken the Light and Love within your four lower bodies until you are physically prepared to ascend with your body. The whole of the physical body has been divinely *blueprinted* or *encoded* to live in Unity Consciousness.

Crucifixion brings you to the point of acknowledging your pain and then asks you to be willing to trust that pain, so that you can use it as your ally. The crucifixion brings you to a crucial point of surrender, or *death,* where you must choose whether or not you are willing to let go of your suffering so that God, as Love, can take you the rest of the way. Love is the ultimate transmuting power. The next chapter describes the Resurrection, which will continue to prepare your mind and body for ascension.

The Resurrection

" ... your light shall break forth like the morning;
Your healing shall spring forth speedily ..."

— Isaiah 58:8

Yᴏᴜʀ I ᴀᴍ Pʀᴇsᴇɴᴄᴇ ɪs ᴀɴᴅʀᴏɢʏɴᴏᴜs, meaning that it is neither male nor female. It is a pure field of love and light used for animating the holographic projection of your individualized expression of Mother / Father God into the world. Your Presence lives and serves within its own vibrational essence on the seventh dimension of your consciousness. It not bound by time, space, or form. Experience has revealed to me that the Presence is now assisting us in expanding into our higher feeling capacities through the feminine aspect of our being, and into our higher thinking capacities through the male aspect of our being. The I AM Presence is projecting both its feminine and its masculine characteristics into the incarnate Christ-self, even though the Presence itself is not limited by gender.

In its female capacity, your Presence sustains your higher feeling nature, forever embracing you in the perfection of God's Love. In its male capacity, the Presence sustains your higher mental nature, forever aligning you with your divine blueprint and your capacities to create using the power of God's Light. The I AM Presence, using the rays of love, light, and intelligence within the three-fold head flame, is continually schooling you in the ways of Unity Consciousness. It does this by filtering its three-fold capacity

51

into the heart, which is encoded to sustain the higher mental body of the Christ-self. The higher mental body then alerts the ego (which coordinates the body-brain complex) that it is to cooperate with you by staying aligned with your divine blueprint. At this point, you may be scratching your head, so I have added the following chart to assist you in *seeing* what I am talking about.

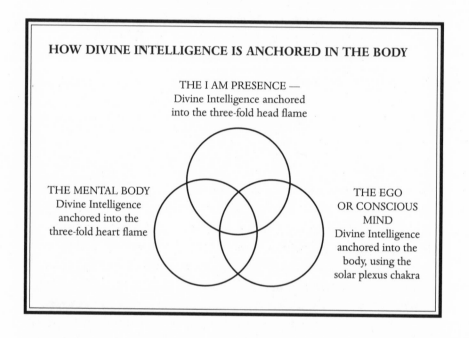

HOW DIVINE INTELLIGENCE IS ANCHORED IN THE BODY

THE I AM PRESENCE —
Divine Intelligence anchored
into the three-fold head flame

THE MENTAL BODY
Divine Intelligence
anchored into the
three-fold heart flame

THE EGO
OR CONSCIOUS
MIND
Divine Intelligence
anchored into the
body, using the
solar plexus chakra

Humanity has primarily been living from the ego-based *will* of the solar plexus. The solar plexus is programmed to help us survive, emotionally and physically, in a third-dimensional world. Your ego now needs to assist you in clearing and lifting the vibrational frequencies of your solar plexus chakra so that it can align your physical body with the fourth dimension. The heart chakra is aligning your higher mental body with your fifth dimensional matrix of consciousness; the throat chakra is aligning you with the sixth dimension; the brow and crown chakras are aligning you with the seventh dimension. At the divine and proper time, the solar plexus will be lifted into the fifth dimension so that your physical body can ascend into Christ Consciousness. At that time, the other chakras will go into their next respective frequency.

> *OUR CHAKRAS ARE ALIGNED*
> *WITH CERTAIN FREQUENCIES,*
> *OR WAVE BANDS OF CONSCIOUSNESS,*
> *ALLOWING US TO BE EMBODIED*
> *AS MULTIDIMENSIONAL BEINGS.*

If enough people succeed in lifting their central focus of power from the solar plexus (the seat of personal will), up to the heart (the seat of love), then we will be able to shift the world consciousness from one of fear and separation to one of love and compassion. This is the first step of our personal and collective resurrection. How long this will take depends on many factors, especially free will. For many years now, we have been witnessing a powerful and wondrous spiritual revolution. To participate in this revolution, a great number of spiritually advanced souls contracted to incarnate on Earth. Many more are still to come.

Many people are beginning to experience clear and precise communications from their I AM Presence, which is always in the Oneness. The beloved Presence sustains and releases divine Light and Love for one's use whenever one is serving God in *any* world of form or in any dimension of being. The Presence maintains Unity Consciousness for us while we are learning or serving on dimensions which may still be founded in duality consciousness.

There is a very definite challenge which every Initiate seems to encounter on the path to God-realization. It occurs in the early stages of interdimensional exploration. The first stratum of non-physical life that one generally encounters is the astral plane. This is the lower fourth dimension and it is the closest to the physical plane. The astral plane is filled with all levels of thought and feeling. It often attracts the emotional and mental bodies by stimulating one's psychic senses. This stimulation is created through phenomena that are simply created out of our thoughts and feelings. The astral plane is like a giant mirror which has enough substance associated with it for us to be able to see, sense, and feel it through our emotional and mental faculties. It is the stuff that many dreams are made of. The astral plane is often the home of those we have loved and known. All in all, it can be a very fascinating place of interest to the interdimensional explorer if one does not have a vision or an experience of the higher dimensions to guide them to seek further.

As ever-awakening souls, we explore each new dimension or level of reality for as long as it continues to give us ways of expanding our awareness. This exploration process keeps us involved in life and interested in our surroundings and each other. As we spiritually evolve, we often become more interested in the subtle planes than we are in the material plane. The Christ Consciousness, however, must be reflected through the whole of one's existence in order that *Thy Kingdom [can] come and Thy Will [can] be done* **on Earth** *as it is in heaven!*

Think how far we have come to be able to coordinate so many different levels of consciousness while still functioning in a physical world! Lately I am noticing that I actually switch from one body of information and consciousness to the next in order to sustain harmony within my being, world, and relationships. We are soon going to realize the truth of ourselves as multidimensional beings who are simultaneously living on many planes of consciousness. I will give you a little practical example of how this works in our everyday lives.

Yesterday I received a disturbing letter. I was writing at the computer when my husband handed me the mail. I was feeling very open and safe since I was in the sanctity of our own home. The letter completely caught me by surprise and *off guard*. I was shocked at how fast my solar plexus went into reactivity. I would like to think that I am beyond this kind of response. I could plainly feel, however, that the emotional and physical body work as a tight, interrelated unit of consciousness and that they were doing what they needed to do to assist me in surviving. It was a wonderful opportunity for me to see if I could lift the lower emotions into the wisdom of the heart while not denying any of my feelings.

My emotional and physical bodies both dropped into fear. They became like little children who have to have their feelings acknowledged. Even though my mind was fine with what was happening, I knew that I needed to let these feelings flow. The rest of my body seemed to be receiving instructions from the solar plexus, until my whole emotional and physical well-being felt threatened. I wanted to use these so-called negative energies to increase my love and understanding.

About an hour later, my husband and I were driving to a gathering. I still felt unsettled within the stomach and solar plexus area of my body. Suddenly these awful energies started shifting within my body. I could feel them lifting into my heart. Suddenly, I started feeling very emotional, so I let myself weep. I found myself thinking of family members who are in pain, and this triggered a whole flood of compassion. Then I began feeling pure, incredible love for no reason at all. We went to a flower stall on the way to the gathering. I felt so fantastic on every level that I immediately went over and hugged the little Vietnamese lady who was selling the flowers. Love became an unstoppable force. You should have seen me at the party!

My initial reaction to the letter actually became the wonderful internal fuel that I needed for lifting the energies within the solar plexus (anger and fear) up into the heart (compassion). I really experienced how we are given the power to transmute and transform dark energy into light. Isn't it fantastic to know that behind every negative emotion there is a positive one? ... always! The next day I wrote a letter in response to the one I had received. It was one of the clearest letters I have ever written. Integrating and staying with my physical, emotional, mental, and spiritual bodies allowed me to access my real thoughts and feelings, and this led to my feeling more unconditional love.

IF ONE DOES NOT MEET THE CHALLENGES OF
THE CONDITIONAL WORLD, ONE MAY MISS
OPPORTUNITIES FOR SPIRITUAL GROWTH.

In the last few years, many of you have been increasing your attunement with the third dimension. You are taking better and better care of your physical bodies. You are also taking more responsibility for removing limiting thoughtforms and patterns out of your etheric bodies. Many of you have healed layers of accumulated dross. Please remember that as you heal your lower bodies, you are also restoring more order and harmony to the astral plane. Through your transformative efforts you are also helping to transmute and release the thoughtforms that have inhibited the freedom of those within your specific family tree.

As we move into this next cycle of our spiritual development, or spiritual rebirth, many are coming into the final *push*. It may be time for you to see and meet the challenges of resurrecting your four lower bodies into their next respective frequencies, or dimensions of consciousness. If you have faced the pain of your separation, passed through at least a good degree of dying to your old self, then you are ready for the resurrection. You have made room for the Holy Spirit to enter into your body more completely, so that it can be resurrected into **several** new frequency wave bands. As your material body becomes increasingly filled with Light, you will begin integrating with your higher Lightbodies, which are the energy fields that make up the other dimensional levels of the Self.

EXPANDING INTO THESE NEW
BODIES OF AWARENESS ASSISTS IN
RESURRECTING THE OLD SELF.

When the higher chakras are opening, we find out that we can operate in other dimensional realities, at least mentally. As mentioned earlier, the astral plane can be an enticing area for exploration, but it is better not to become enmeshed in its attractions, since they are so heavily penetrated by humanity's limiting thoughts and feelings. Astral substance responds to us by forming pictures around our projected thoughts. It is an area where we can manifest a certain amount of reality. This illusionary substance encourages many to believe that what they are feeling and seeing is illumined truth. The astral plane is the most dense of the subtle worlds, and it has the most impact on our physical senses. Nightmares are a good example of the lower astral plane's effect on our third-dimensional bodies.

THOUGHT CREATES EVERY WORLD IN THE COSMOS. WE ARE MAGNETIZED TO WORLDS THAT MATCH OUR THOUGHTS.

Please be aware that the astral plane has been created by the thoughts and feelings of humanity. It is also filled with those who are waiting to return to Earth. Since we are often connected to past friends and relatives who are, indeed, wanting to come back to this planet, I highly recommend testing ALL entities who present themselves to you as friends or Masters. You may do this by saying something like the following: *I greet thee and honor the Christ of thy Presence. Do you wish to communicate with me in the Light of the Christ?* If there is no response, then it is a great gift to the entity to call forth their I AM Presence and guardian angel and ask them to take the entity to a place of learning that is in alignment with their divine blueprint. It is always good practice to test interdimensional entities before aligning yourself with their energies, even when you think you are in contact with Christ-conscious beings.

There are disincarnate entities on the astral plane who like to establish relationships with those who are still embodied. These disincarnate beings feel incomplete with their life on Earth and often feel that they can keep on living through others. Many who "pass over" remain attached to their homes, families, and favorite *haunts*. If they were especially fond of drinking alcohol, for example, they might still be hanging out at a local bar. Since these beings do not know how to source the true Light and Power of God, they use the light of incarnate beings as their source.

Your I AM Presence is in direct resonance with all of those who have already ascended, as well as those who are known as the *Elohim*.[17] Heart Initiates are tested to see how they define and use energy long before they are allowed to manifest their greater powers as Christed beings within a physical world. If you are guided to serve others as a representative for the Spiritual Hierarchy, you will have to learn how to increasingly infuse your thoughts, words, and actions with as much Light and Love as possible. Our actions are constantly being reviewed by our own Higher Selves and by our spiritual guardians to keep us from accruing any unnecessary karma.

Twice a year, by an act of God's Grace, we formally meet with the Spiritual Hierarchy on the inner planes to examine our soul's progress. The more conscious we become, the more involved we can be in objectively viewing our own lives. I have experienced the Ascended Masters in their Flame, Opalescent, and Diamond Lightbodies, which would be their *forms* of expression (for me, at least) in the fifth, sixth, and seventh dimensions respectively. It is my understanding that the Ascended Masters and Cosmic Beings primarily *live* on the sixth and seventh dimensions, and that they only occasionally manifest themselves in the fourth or the fifth dimension so that we can really *feel* their love and physically *receive* their illumination into our subtle anatomy. I have been enveloped in such an exquisite exchange of indescribable energy that my whole body has been consumed in Love and Light. During those times, I have occasionally disappeared from physical sight, only to return a few moments later.

---

[17] A body of Conscious Beings who are responsible for creating worlds and systems of worlds.

The emotional body has been living in the confines of its lower nature for many thousands of years. It is more than ready to be revived (resurrected) from its previous state in order to ascend (or expand) into its next higher body of consciousness. As we ascend, all of our lower bodies are shifting progressively into more refined states of being. These bodies are each moving into the dimensional frequencies that are to be their new home. The present goal of my lower emotional body, which is seated in the solar plexus, is to be aligned with the true love nature of the Christ-self in the fifth dimension.

The chakras are lifting the four lower bodies into progressively higher dimensions. I have been guided to stabilize the first twelve dimensions within my chakras and DNA system. This will fully align the I AM Presence, also known as the Monad, with the thirteenth chakra. This center or chakra is the bridge to the multi-dimensional energy systems within our higher bodies. It also attunes us to our Cosmic Monad, which functions as an overself to the I AM Presence. The Cosmic Monad serves in accordance with the divine blueprint for the multi-universes.

REMEMBER, WHEN YOU INVOKE YOUR I AM PRESENCE

OR YOUR COSMIC MONAD,

YOU ARE ALSO INVOKING ITS DIVINE BLUEPRINT.

Even though I am aware of accessing information from the higher dimensions, I feel that a major part of my focus must remain on bringing the *mind* of my lower bodies into Unity or Christ Consciousness. It is my understanding that full-body ascension actually depends on all chakras and interdimensional Lightbodies becoming unified with the heart. Heart refers here to a wide band of energy that spans from the thymus, in the center of the upper chest, to the end of the sternum in the "V" of the rib cage. The three-fold heart flame within this region of the body is encoded with Christ Consciousness so that it may spiritually qualify the incoming energies that it receives from the lower chakras.

The heart flame is programmed to transform all pre-existing and incoming energy into love, wisdom and power, allowing one to continually build and magnify the Christ vibration. This happens naturally when the chakras are operating in harmony with the soul. If one's energies are held in denial for too long, then they eventually get blocked in such a way that the life force begins collecting too much "red" or even "black" energy at the base of the spine. This makes it nearly impossible for the incarnate soul to feel the bliss which naturally occurs when the ascending and descending currents are running unimpeded. The stored or denied energies which have been stored at the base of the spine are why the kundalini in the majority of humankind has remained imprisoned or dormant. If there are too many discordant or denied energies within one's body, then the ascending and descending currents cannot flow through the etheric nerve channels and the heart flame cannot do its job.

One of the functions of the resurrection is to bring one's optimal feeling capacity *back to life*. When the three lower chakras are fully aligned with your heart flame, you will begin *sensing* and *feeling* the Christ frequency of divine love throughout your body. Your three-fold heart flame is encoded by your own higher intelligence to be the receiving and transmitting station for all the energies that are constantly ascending and descending throughout your body. These magnificent ascending and descending currents are a part of the greater kundalini energies of Mother/Father God. As they unite and flow through the nerve channels of your being, you will literally begin to feel how the divine Love and Light of the Creator is continually sustaining the relationship between your physical and spiritual bodies.

The heart is the great intermediary between your upper and lower chakras. Your chakras are connected by three major nerve channels (*nadis*) within your etheric body. These channels are termed the *ida* or *idakalai*, the *pingala* and the *susumna*,[18] and they carry the kundalini energies through your body. You will be able to receive and emit more of the Light and Love of the Holy Spirit when these great currents are running freely within your body. Your connection to the cosmos is through the kundalini, which is meant to pulsate in and through your spiritual energy centers spontaneously, without trauma or drama. This can and will happen when your chakras are cleared and your ego has agreed to cooperate in your ascension.

It takes a lot of wisdom, intention, and love to sustain the true vibration of the Christ at the heart while living within the influence of other peoples thoughts and feelings, especially during this purification cycle. Discordant forcefields and disharmonious environments are testing us on a daily basis. It is important to remember that everything and everyone is coming into your life to help you ascend, and to free you from your past patterning. The desire for union with the Divine is the deepest longing of an Initiate's heart. It is the eternal "juice" that has kept us going life after life.

---

[18] The *ida* is the lunar nerve channel representing the divine feminine. It is on the left side of the spine. The *pingala* is the solar nerve channel representing the divine masculine. It regulates the flow of heat on the right side of the *susumna*, which is the central nadi in the spinal cord.

Interdimensional Retreats

"But they who wait for the Lord shall renew their strength; they shall grow wings as a dove; they shall run and not be weary; and they shall walk and not faint." [19]

— Isaiah 40:31

Aʟʟ ꜰᴏʀᴍ ᴡᴏʀʟᴅꜱ, physical and etheric, are the product of our projected thoughts and feelings. The heavenly worlds on the (higher) fourth and fifth dimensions have been created by the refined thoughts and feelings of the Ascended Masters and Cosmic Beings. They have manifested etheric temples, retreats, and schools on these dimensions so that we can go there to learn more about ourselves and our processes as Initiates of the Heart.

Although we are generally unconscious of going to school on the inner planes, we are, nevertheless, actively serving and learning as much in our subtle bodies as we are in our physical bodies. Although our nights are often filled with a conglomeration of dis-associated thoughts, feelings, and actions, there is much going on that we do not see or remember. We are sometimes graced with consciously working with our Master Teachers on the inner planes. Although I sometimes find myself in an typical classroom setting, my teachers often present their lessons using thought projections. I am asked to either walk into or witness a living, moving scene.

---

[19] *Holy Bible from the Ancient Eastern Text.* George M. Lamsa translation from the Aramaic of the Peshitta.

Holograms can be projected by the Masters without the use of a screen. However, in the Royal Teton Retreat, where the Karmic Review Boards come together every January and July, there is a very large, dark blue wall that is often used as a viewing screen. Our Ascended Master sponsors use this velvet-like screen for showing us present or past life scenes that need to be more clearly understood in the light of our desire to spiritually evolve and eventually ascend. Although these inner plane lessons often take place during the night, the experiences that we have in the presence of our Master Teachers are not like regular dreams.

When you become aware of your ongoing Christ Process and aware of working with your teachers, then you often become more consciously involved in your own evolution. As the Initiate continues to evolve, then his or her Ascended Master guides can more easily assist them in being drawn up into a more conscious alignment with their Christ-self during the night. It is during our sleep that much healing and clearing is accomplished. Sometimes the results of your night's learning will flood into your conscious mind upon awakening. If you allow yourself to lie in that state between waking and sleeping for awhile, much of this information can become available to your conscious mind.

Interdimensional schools and retreats act as bridges for supplying us with the education that we need for awakening. By the grace of our celestial hosts, we are being shown how we consciously serve ourselves and others within and beyond the limitations of the form worlds. Inner plane lessons are giving us the Cosmic Laws that we use for manifesting ourselves as free beings.

Eventually one begins accessing the higher-dimensional retreats where Cosmic Beings invite us to enter into even more expanded states of learning and being. Within these realms, our chakras are aligned with the frequencies of our higher Lightbodies. Glorious beings of radiant Light and Love teach us how to so perfectly balance our mental and emotional natures that we no longer experience conflict or extreme energy pulls between our higher and lower natures. Here we are trained to bring our energy centers (chakras) into such divine Love and Light that we can shift our bodies into one radiant sphere of unified conscious intelligence. It is here that we learn how to go between the worlds of form and formlessness, and how to shift from individual to collective consciousness. All of this is part of our training for serving in the higher dimensions.

As we move into the more subtle regions of the cosmos, the substance is lighter and the language of Light and Love is expressed within an almost blinding white fire substance, denoting the frequency of the I AM Presence in its cosmic capacity. This aspect of the Presence is known as the Cosmic Monad and it uses white fire to support the substance that makes up all of your higher Lightbodies. I will be referring to the Christ and the Cosmic Christ as offices within the Spiritual Hierarchy, as well as levels of consciousness to which we are individually attuned.

You have a Christ-self which is anchored into your individualized soul in the three-fold flame of your heart. Your Christ-self is connected to your I AM Presence, which is generally anchored in the three-fold flame of your head (within the Holy of Holies). Many people I have been working with lately are starting to bring the light of their I AM Presence into the center of their three-fold heart flame, allowing the Christ and the Presence to become one within the heart. At this point, the dimensional frequencies that are encoded to operate the consciousness within each of your twelve chakras are going to start preparing your body to receive the vibrations of your Great Central Sun White Fire Body, which is attuned to *Cosmic* Christ Consciousness.

In other words, when your I AM Presence descends from the Holy of Holies into your heart, it leaves a vacancy in your three-fold *head* flame which is gradually going to be filled by the consciousness (light) and essence (love) of your Cosmic Monad. This needs to happen in stages, so that you are not too overwhelmed with the new energies. The timing of these stages depends on your body's ability to handle the vibrations of many new dimensional frequencies that will be coming through your new chakras, each of which will be progressively aligned with your crown chakra. Each of these chakras will initiate you into ever-expanding expressions of your Cosmic Consciousness. These spiritual energy centers are continually aligning your body with the love, light, and wisdom of your White Fire Body — the vehicle that was used to express your first individualization from out of the Great Central Sun.

When your Cosmic Monad aligns with your Holy of Holies in your three-fold head flame, it becomes your teacher, just as your Monad or I AM Presence is also your teacher. These two primary monitors (your Monad and your Cosmic Monad) live, learn, and serve with many other teachers, known to us as Ascended Masters and Cosmic Beings. We do communicate with these beings in the Interdimensional Retreats, but more often we are trained by them while we are serving here on Earth. This is especially true during this cycle of our evolution. This relationship is sometimes an unconscious one, meaning that the incarnate server is often unaware of receiving instructions from its spiritual overseers, but it is happening nonetheless.

Although we are gradually being awakened into our capacities as Ascended Masters and Cosmic Beings, we need to be reminded of this when we are serving within the density of a dual-mind world. Hence, the Spiritual Hierarchy continues to open our channels of remembrance while we are serving here on Earth. Your I AM Presence and your Cosmic Monad are encoded to assist them by sustaining the template of your inheritance within the many realms and dimensions of the One Being.

We are being trained to enter and serve within many different vibrational frequencies. As we progressively expand into the greater Self, we are individually and collectively awakening within the many ocataves of consciousness that sustain the planets, the stars, the solar system, the galaxy, the universe, and the multi-universes within the extended cosmos. We have always been a part of these greater bodies of consciousness. We will continue to expand into greater and greater levels of service and joy, as we reawaken the full spectrum of our White Fire Body as it was originally *birthed* from Source. By the Grace of God, I have been a witness.

The Aura

"Let your light so shine before all, that they may see your good works and glorify your Father who art in heaven."
— Matthew 5:16

T HE AURA CONTAINS THE COLORED AND NEARLY COLORLESS LIGHT that makes up the subtle energy fields around one's body. These energy matrixes begin by reflecting the emanations of the etheric body, and end by reflecting the emanations of one's White Fire Body (described in the previous chapter). The auric fields around one's body are the light waves that are being emitted by all the many dimensional frequencies of the Self. Each of these fields is aligned to specific musical tones and colors, until the sounds become inaudible, and there is no longer color (as we generally perceive it).

We are constantly awakening, or being awakened, to embrace larger and larger fields of love and light. These *fields* are what I am referring to as dimensions. As we progressively expand into the living intelligence of each new dimension, our auras reflect this expansion. We express ourselves through our aura according to how awakened we are within our planetary, solar, galactic, universal, and cosmic heritage. This does not mean that one has to be constantly aware of living and serving on every dimension in order to emanate a beautiful, expanded aura. Whenever one is attuned to the Self as Love, the aura expresses beauty, peace, harmony, and all of the other attributes of Unity Consciousness.

We all come from the same Source and are always equal within the One Heart.[20] The first layers of the aura, however, reflect the individualized and varied ways that each of us might mentally and emotionally respond or react to the same situation. The aura demonstrates one's ability to direct and sustain energy in a pattern. I have seen a man think of love and create a very beautiful aura that literally demonstrated love; then he held the thought of clarity and the aura became absolutely crystalline and jewel-like in its emanation. Through the use of Kirlian photography, I got to see that beautiful auras can be created by one's thoughts and feelings. Although I have never seen it photographed, I know that one's aura can also be positively or negatively affected by the projected thoughts and feelings of others.

It may be important to note that the aura can be consciously retracted or pulled in towards the body when one chooses to be less expanded or vulnerable to outside forces. One may also place a seal of protection around the whole of the self, at least six feet in every direction, in order to sustain the integrity of one's energy systems. The aura actually contracts when we sense danger. Whenever I have been awakened in the middle of the night by strange noises, I feel my aura automatically seal up the back of my spine as it contracts in towards my body. Our subtle bodies can be just as abused or hurt as our physical bodies can. The glandular system is programmed to alert us when we are moving into energy fields that are not supportive of our well being.

As Initiates expand into the higher dimensions, their auras begin drawing in greater and greater amounts of Love and Light. This amplification not only adds to one's personal aura, but also to the auric fields surrounding the planet. Even though we generally cannot see auras, we are always intuitively sensing them. We are each — consciously and unconsciously — attracted or repelled by the quality of Love and Light within another's aura. The first four layers of the aura are created by the emanations of the physical,

---

[20] Refers to being in Oneness with the Heart of the Creator.

etheric, emotional, and mental bodies — in that order. The etheric body holds the divine blueprints for the physical, emotional, and mental bodies. It is also the interface between the corporeal and subtle bodies. The fifth layer of the aura is generated by what is being called a *Lightbody*. At this level of the Self, one begins to align with Unity or Christ Consciousness at the heart. As the aura expands out into progressive layers of decreasing density, each one is attuned to specific frequencies of intelligence called *Lightbodies*.

True avatars, who live in full God-realization, *embody* the divine blueprint within every body they occupy while they are serving on the Earth. Jesus reflected the purity of a Christed being while he was within a human form so that we would have a standard for living mastery after he left. He showed us not only how to live, but also how to resurrect oneself and ascend into freedom. We have the opportunity to show him that we love him enough to live his example, not merely to understand it.

All Heart Initiates have the potential for reflecting and emanating the purity, the love, the power, and the wisdom of their full potential self through their auric fields. On the fifth, sixth, and seventh dimensions, beings have only shown themselves to me in their androgynous forms. Fifth density [21] bodies seem to be composed of a flowing, opalescent-like substance, slightly colored with very soft hues. Sixth and seventh density bodies appear to be made out of diamond-like particles of light which are extremely bright. I am still learning about these interdimensional bodies, and I can only give you a hint at what these really look like from my experiences.

There seems to be no real aura, per se, around higher-dimensional beings. They appear to be existing in one whole spectrum of light, with no distinct differences between their form aspect and their spiritual aspect. I think the term *Whole Lightbody* is going to become increasingly meaningful to us in the days ahead. Cosmic Beings express God's perfection within an indefinable field of Love, permeated with only the very purest essence of God-Light.

---

[21] "Density" is synonymous with "dimensional."

When vibrationally resonating within the energy fields of these Divine Beings, you soon discover that we have only experienced an incredibly small fraction of the pure, unconditional love that is available to us.

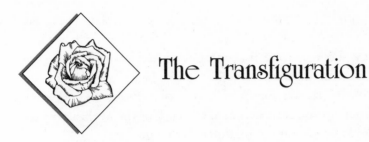

The Transfiguration

The "Transfiguration" is the full coming into form of the Christ that you are, unbound by mass consciousness and unfettered by human addictions.

WHEN THE HOLY SPIRIT starts integrating with the physical and emotional bodies, then the *Transfiguration* begins in earnest. The Initiate will literally feel the changes taking place, rather than just know *about* them. The cells of the physical body will be quickened as they receive more and more of the pure Light substance of the immortal Self. You will be living and, indeed, walking in a field of Love and Light that is no longer limited by the flesh body or the dual mind.

The heart has been seeded by the Spiritual Hierarchy in agreement with one's own I AM Presence to vibrate in an atmosphere of unconditional love. This state of total love, however, has to be joined with the wisdom and the power of the higher mental body[22] in order for one to begin the Transfiguration part of the Christ Process. One's ego must move into perfect alignment with the three basic aspects of the heart flame — love, wisdom, and power — since it is only from the seed of the Christ within the heart that one can merge with Divine Will (which is centered at the throat chakra and the back of the skull).

---

[22] The part of the "mind" that lives in perfect relationship with the "heart" consciousness of the Christ-self.

The throat chakra is a place of testing. It is the place of the last battle between the human and divine aspects of the Self. It is where personal will comes to terms with Divine Will. It is also here that one is given the full spiritual ability to manifest using the "spoken word." During the purification of the solar plexus, many people experience pain and contraction at the back of the neck, across the shoulder blades, and at the medulla oblongata.

The higher mind is created through the full awakening and blossoming of the sacred relationship that exists between the pineal, pituitary, hypothalamus, thyroid, and thymus glands. This represents one's ability to access and sustain a proper balance between the following chakras: the brow (pituitary), the crown (pineal), the eighth chakra (hypothalamus), the throat (thyroid), and the heart (thymus). As the wisdom of the heart trains one to consciously balance the relationship between the higher and lower chakras, one is given the power to co-create with the Elohim and the Ascended Masters, thus assisting in the transfiguration on every level of the Self.

During the Transfiguration, you will probably find yourself merging with the beauty of your surroundings. When you look at something, you will enter into it while experiencing the pleasure of your union. Everything will be increasingly intensified, both the pain and the pleasure. Colors will be brighter and sounds will either be more exquisite or more discordant. You may find yourself becoming more discerning as you learn how to choose the objects of your contemplation. You may wonder where you have been all of your life!

You will be experiencing the third dimension from a whole new perspective, and in that sense you will be living in a *new* world. You may find that the nerve endings of your body occasionally feel as though they are extended endlessly into space. It can be alarming at first to experience Oneness with all life and to realize that it has been there all along! To sustain your sanity and your Oneness, you must remain anchored in unconditional love and yet balance that love with wisdom and power in the manifest world. It takes a lot of mastery to do this. It is definitely an ongoing process.

The Transfiguration can begin on a more conscious level when you are fully embodying the pure spiritual essence of the God I AM. It is always helpful to maintain purity in your relationships by remaining impeccably honest. You may wish to ask your friends and relatives to release their unspoken thoughts and feelings about you and your past actions. Though often painful and difficult, honesty has the power to crumble the walls of separation and to heal the past.

The human ego forever plays on one's weaknesses or one's desire for power and control. This can take many, many forms, depending on past patterning. Be forever loving and patient with your magnificent and beloved Self. Always remember that you are a multidimensional being who is at once both human and divine. We are now in a time where we can heal the many thousands of years of separation from God and from each other, and we are literally merging the heavenly worlds with our lives here on Earth!

We are bringing God to Earth by *ascending* in consciousness beyond the physical and the astral planes, in order to reclaim our freedom as true spiritual beings. We are also *descending* by bringing the consciousness of the Christ-self into the physical world, thus transforming ourselves and our bodies by increasing the light within our bodies and environments. This is an incredible undertaking and one that has never been done by so many people at one time. Be gentle and kind, joyous and forgiving, with yourself and others. We are all consciously or unconsciously striving to become divinely human on a planet which is, after all, a Garden of Eden in the heavens of this universe!

Since these are the times that we are being challenged to fully embody the Christ-self, the Transfiguration is what many Initiates will be focusing on during this decade of our transformation. As this *Feminine Ray Age*[23] enfolds us in the arms of birth, we are realizing more and more how we have actually been preparing for thousands of years to receive the Holy Spirit into every cell of our being. As we enter the next spiral of creation, or the Feminine Ray Age, we are being released from the wheel of karma, birth, death, and reincarnation. Some will be leaving the Earth to become inter-galactic emissaries, where they will serve as Cosmic Beings who have full multidimensional freedom within at least this system of worlds. Some are sincerely desiring to return to this planet in order to assist in creating the next Golden Age. Others may have started something on the material plane which they deeply desire to complete. And still others are waiting to be reincarnated onto other planets which are better suited to their present level of development.

> *"For lo, the winter is past, the rain is over and gone, the flowers appear on the Earth; the time of pruning has come, and the voice of the turtledove is heard in our land."*

— Song of Solomon 2:11,12
(*The Holy Bible*, Lamsa translation)

---

[23] Feminine Ray Age describes our present cycle of unfoldment since it so clearly defines our current need to enter into the emotional or *feminine* recesses of the self. It does not imply gender.

The Ascension

*"Enter by the narrow gate, for wide is the gate and broad is
the way that leads to destruction, and there are many who go
in by it. Because narrow is the gate and difficult is the way
which leads to life, and there are few who find it."*

— Matthew 7:13,14

The Holy Spirit awakens the Christ Flame that is seeded
within our hearts so that we will have the love, the wisdom, and
the power that we need to resurrect the human self. Although we
are constantly being supported by the Ascended Masters and their
angels, only the Flame of the Christ within our hearts can set us
free and prepare us for the journey home to God. We must forever
sustain the pure vision of our ascension within our minds and hearts,
if that is our desire. This is not a selfish desire. The universal Law of
Love declares our divine right to live in eternal union with God.

The only power which can finally return us into the pure Light
of God is love. Our cells are either expanding in love or contracting
in fear. The ego-body-mind is programmed to survive, and it feels
fear when it is threatened. The ego will continue to sabotage us
until we understand its role in our lives. Even with understanding,
it does take courage to release and transmute the thoughts and
feelings that continue to support fear. Bodily fear is a natural
response to attack, but we can even realize our dominion in the
face of danger or death. To ascend is to face the unknown. When
we transition, it will make it easier if we can surrender to God with
a love that is absolute.

FEAR AND PAIN INDICATE RESISTANCE TO LOVE AND TO SURRENDERING TO GOD.

We must fully develop and abide within the consciousness of our Master Self *before* we make our final ascension from the Earth plane. When all of the chakras are healed and karmically cleared, at least to a great degree, then Heart Initiates become wayshowers, teachers, and healers, just by their inner attunement with the Christ. Lightworkers are generally inspired by the Spirit of their I AM Presence to perform some kind of service in the world. This allows Initiates to test their power and their resolve to physically manifest as a Christ while bringing the healing energies of unconditional love into the world.

Each one of us truly knows if our heart is resonating with our I AM Presence. When we are living in union with God, compassion floods our body and a sense of lightness and well-being prevails. Compassion and concern for humanity's plight increases as your heart expands. If heaviness or sadness re-enters your heart, then just know that another layer of pain is making itself known. This is actually a great blessing, so do not be dismayed when there seems no end to your unfolding.

Due to the density of the mass consciousness at this time, it takes a very powerful Initiate to truly avoid merging with the suffering of this planet. It is important to continually develop and demonstrate compassion, but it is not necessary to become weighed down by the suffering of the world. It helps to know what is really yours to transmute and what belongs to somebody else. People need to deeply experience the inner strength and true self-love that it takes to bring *themselves* into the Light.

During your journey, you will be led to others who are in resonance with your level of unfolding. You will assist each other by your very association. Each of us is very carefully tracked by our spiritual overseers and by our own I AM Presence so that we find soulmates who will help us remember. When you do locate the people with whom you are in spiritual harmony, there will be no doubt of their precious place in your life. In their presence, you will feel more love because they will assist you in expanding your emotional and physical alignment with the I AM Presence. This will bring the physical expression of God as the One Self into a more personalized context and increase your faith in life here on Earth.

THERE IS ALWAYS

A CONSTANT REFINING TAKING PLACE,

WHICH MEANS THAT WE MUST OFTEN GO DEEPER

IN ORDER TO GO HIGHER.

This particular incarnation is allowing a great number of Lightworkers the opportunity to consciously ascend out of the limitations of the lower-dimensional self. As one enters into the freedom of the unlimited Self, spiritual responsibility becomes greater. Initiates frequently become teachers, where they risk being worshiped or idealized as gurus. It is important to remember that all physical plane teachers are themselves advancing. Teachers usually attract students who can truly benefit from their teachings, and when students stop resonating with their teachers, they generally move on unless a personal attachment has been created. When and if this happens, the teacher may have to gently release the student.

MAJOR INITIATIONS ONLY OCCUR

THROUGH THE GRACE OF GOD.

Teachers can greatly assist us by describing certain parts of their own initiatic processes. They can also help in raising the frequencies of a room by their own vibrational essence and attunement to the Christ vibration. Shifts in consciousness often take place when an entire group is being overlit by the energy matrix of the Cosmic Christ. With focus and intention, facilitators can often lead a group in creating a resonant field of Love and Light into which an

Ascended Master or Cosmic Being can come and quicken the hearts of all those ready to receive.

True and lasting initiations can occur directly through the I AM Presence of a physical plane master or an avatar if a student is spiritually prepared to move into a higher state of consciousness. Initiations are given and received when the chakras and the energy systems within the four lower bodies are ready to receive an additional influx of Love and Light. Sometimes it would *appear* that you have done all that you can to prepare for an initiation, and still it does not happen according to your expectations. You are always advancing to the next stage of your spiritual development according to a timing that is determined by your divine blueprint.

One of the purest initiations you can receive comes from your own beloved I AM Presence. Sometimes a divine merging with your God-Presence happens in the early morning hours, when you are in a Grace-filled state of being. When your Presence descends into your sight, this is initiatic in and of itself. If you are fortunate enough to be embraced by your Presence, then your body will be filled with such Love and Light that you will know that God has personally come to pay you a visit. You will become so filled with the ecstasy of Divine Love that you may enter into a state of pure rapture. In this exquisite union with the Essence of the Holy Spirit, you will be receiving Divine Wisdom on a cellular level.

Much of this illumination will be directly assimilated by your cells as Light encodings. There it becomes internal knowing, to be called forth when necessary. Some information, however, is filtered through the mind's resources, which are amazingly vast! The quality and quantity of the reference banks obviously vary with every soul's present and past life experiences. You have most probably experienced innumerable lives on other planets, stars, and dimensions of being. We each have access to an entire cellular library of accumulated knowledge. We can also find answers to our questions by calling forth the Libraries of Light within the greater Akasha, which contain the universal and cosmic memory banks of the collective mind. *Ask and ye shall receive!*

All stages of the Christ Process are actually occurring simultaneously, just as all levels of the multidimensional self are living simultaneously within their own vibrational spheres of life. It takes time to integrate those parts of ourselves which have been in dormancy. When we drop into the patterns of the past, it appears as though we start the Christ Process all over again! We must be patient with God's divine timing. Though one stage may take a particularly long time, another stage may go very rapidly.

After the lower self, also referred to as the inner child or the human self, is recognized and loved free, then greater dominion will be given to your Christ-self. Initiates soon learn that it is to their advantage to accept complete responsibility for their thoughts and actions.

In order to ascend into the full potential of your Master Self, the incarnate human expression of that Self must fully harmonize the masculine Light of Divine Intelligence with the feminine Love of the Holy Spirit.

Part Two

CLAIMING
YOUR
FREEDOM

# Claiming Your Freedom

WHEN THERE IS A SUSPENSION OF ALL CHERISHED BELIEFS and memories, there is a precious moment of vulnerability that most people will not allow themselves to feel. Vulnerability is the door to true freedom, and when it comes, the moment is very precious. Most people squander it; they don't realize how precious it really is.

To claim your freedom on the physical plane, you must be willing to be vulnerable and, therefore, to heal the roots of your separation. It is not necessary to pick up your sword or to become a spiritual warrior. It is not a time to engage in the battle of the sexes, or any kind of war between the dark and the light forces of creation. As a race, we have been carrying the sword instead of speaking the word by truly making the call for our freedom. Only a very small percentage of the population has any idea of what it means to live in the joy of real spiritual freedom. However, the numbers are increasing and many are being reborn or reawakened into their original knowing. We have always been given the free will to find our way back home.

MOST PEOPLE DO NOT CONSCIOUSLY DESIRE
TO BE LIFTED OUT OF THE DRAMA
THAT EXISTS ON THE THIRD DIMENSION.

Even after one gets a taste of Christ Consciousness, they must really remained focused to sustain that consciousness. It takes a strong heart and mind not be magnetized back into the emotional excitement that sustains the duality play of the third dimension. Initiates are often attracted back into the drama of competition, jealousy, judgment, and other separative thoughts and feelings. The ego has had dominion for thousands of years. The maligned ego is the only real devil we will ever have to face, and we can do this by realizing the vital part it has played in bringing us into our individuation. It has protected us, and allowed us to survive during thousands of years of darkness. It must now be embraced into the Heart, so that it, too, can be brought out of separation.

One will usually not be able to permanently rise out of living from the lower nature until there is a burning and absolute desire to be free. This is a momentous time in our history, a time when many will want to understand more about their own sacredness. We are reclaiming our spiritual birthright by returning to the Heart and by cutting out the roots of everything that is sustaining our separation. Cutting these roots of dependency on the old self and on the old way of being in the world is the most challenging part of the Christ Process.

Claiming your freedom can be at once ecstatic and painful. You must love yourself enough to "be there" for yourself through the full birthing process. It may takes years or months, depending on how willing you are to let go the attachments of your ego and your illusions about who you think you are or should be. We cannot afford to accrue any more personal or planetary karma by supporting that which is limiting our movement into a new conscious level of freedom.

We each have a very specific and individualized way of freeing ourselves. Although there are roles to play that assist both personal and planetary freedom, and it is wonderful to realize that you even have a part in the play, you will discover that eternal joy comes from living simply as your True Self. That realization comes as a great moment in your spiritual evolvement, for it is in that moment that the persona is lost, vulnerability is there, and you are free. It is not your role that is really important; it is the permission you give to yourself to be unattached to your role and, therefore, completely vulnerable as the newborn self within every moment.

The Astral Plane

We have the power and the responsibility to change the vibrational quality of the astral world by changing the quality of our thoughts.

INSTEAD OF LIVING FROM OUR HEART and embodying the vibrational frequency of Divine Love, humankind has been floundering in an ever-turbulent sea of misqualified thoughts.[24] That sea is always pulsing between negative and positive polarities. It is commonly called the *astral plane,* and it penetrates all of life in the third dimension. The belief systems that support duality are subliminally affecting everyone; they will continue to do so until people truly understand that they can change the subtle energies that constitute the astral environment which *lives* within and around this world. By qualifying our thoughts, we can choose to live beyond the conflict and the confusion that exists on the lower octaves of the astral plane. We can also help to clear these octaves by invoking the assistance of the celestial hosts of the archangels and the Elohim. They can and do assist us in transmuting and lifting negative energies (and the entities often associated with them) back into their original divine Light substance.

Over many thousands of years, the inhabitants of this beloved world have encased the Earth in an astral web, created by threads

---

[24] Thoughts not created in harmony with Divine Love or Wisdom.

of energy wound into what are called *thoughtforms*. Astral and psychic thoughtforms are woven out of both our limited and our unlimited thoughts and feelings. They are constantly being expanded and attracted to one another due to the similarity of their vibrations. The internal regions of the Earth receive our body's discharged energies. Our creations, therefore, penetrate the planetary body, permeating it with astral energies. I have traveled with the angels through the volcanic tubes of the Earth and witnessed the astral density that exists inside the planet. We have been given the dominion to work with angels and/or to call them forth to assist us in clearing the astral energies, in both the inner and the outer *atmospheres* of Earth.

Special dispensations of the Spiritual Hierarchy are granting us the grace of being served by thousands upon thousands of those within the celestial hosts of the Elohim who are presently assisting us in learning how to align with the higher *mental* capacities of the Christ-self, and the celestial hosts of the archangels (who are presently assisting us in living from the heart and the higher *feeling* nature of the Christ-self). This is greatly accelerating the ascension process.

We are constantly sending thoughts and feelings into the auric matrix of our environment and into the subtle energy fields of all those with whom we come in contact. Thoughtforms are then layered into vibrational octaves of love and light, or fear and darkness. They literally gravitate to the energy fields to which they are attuned. Each octave corresponds to a level of consciousness, commonly referred to as a dimension, and each dimension consists of twelve octaves, or tonal qualities, within itself.

The astral plane penetrates both the third and fourth dimensions. The more dense the thoughts and the more disharmonious the feelings, the closer they are to the physical plane and the more apt they are to be re-conceived and manifested back into the world of form. The lower strata of the Earth's aura, both around and within the planet herself, are filled with the dense, limiting thoughtforms and fear-based feelings which make up much of the mass consciousness.

THE ASTRAL PLANE IS
THE FIRST DOOR WE PASS THROUGH
IN THE ASCENSION PROCESS.
IT MUST BE UNDERSTOOD AND MASTERED
IF WE ARE TO ENTER INTO THE FREEDOM OF
CHRIST CONSCIOUSNESS.

Both our negative and positive thoughts and feelings pulse and *live* as thoughtforms in the vibrational field to which they are attuned. Our more refined thoughts and feelings are attracted to the higher dimensions. *Our personal auras always reflect where we are living in our minds.* If someone is thinking angry thoughts, for example, then the colors and thoughtforms that are associated with anger would be in that person's aura. Thoughts of love and harmony also create a corresponding color, sound, and thought matrix within one's aura. Since most of us cannot see or *read* auras, we have a lot of privacy. However, extrasensory capacities are becoming more commonplace and soon there will actually be much less of this privacy. Often we get mixed messages from people, and that is an indication that the aura you are actually *sensing* is not matching the words you are hearing.

The astral plane is made up of a crystalline-type substance that sustains the living *pictures* we feed into it. These pictures keep supporting our inherited beliefs until we decide to change the thoughts. Our cities and countries are encased in spheres of subtle energies which have been created by the thoughtforms of their inhabitants. Every town, just like every home, is surrounded by the vibrational energy field that makes up the collective consciousness of those who live there.

Our beloved Earth was created out of the Love and Light substance of God by those who are called the Elohim. These mighty builders, or creator gods, are capable of sustaining such pure thought and feeling that they can manifest worlds and systems of worlds for the Creator. By living on a physical plane, we are learning what it means to be responsible creators. Here we are able to *hear* and *see* and *touch* what it is we are manifesting into our lives and worlds. We have been training to become more *conscious* co-creators.

Movies and television have tremendous visual and sound impact on our emotional, mental, and physical bodies. Our subconscious is greatly affected by music and media and, as far as I can see, we are presently being exposed to all kinds of negative influences. As the lower octaves of the astral plane are being cleared, we are seeing every hidden aspect of the collective consciousness coming forth in living sound, picture, and color. It is a time for great discernment. Complete exposure of the negative forces is actually to be expected during a purification cycle. The effect of this exposure, however, is testing all of us and especially our children. Pray for their alignment with the Light, and know that all is really in Divine Order. Many of the young are strong and wonderfully advanced in their knowing.

BY CHOICE, WE ARE EXERCISING WHAT IT IS
WE WANT TO NOURISH WITHIN OUR AURAS
AND WITHIN THE PLANET'S AURA.

We are being given the opportunity of creating a whole new reality base — one that is founded on the art of mindfulness. This challenge clearly demands that we remain awake and aware of what we are creating moment by moment. This may sound difficult, but the challenge is there as a part of the opportunity. The Holy Breath is a gift of God's pure energy. We have been given the free will to qualify God's energy by our consciousness. **What we focus upon, we bring into the world.**

BEING MINDFUL IS BEING PRESENT:
IT IS LIVING WITH FULL BODY, MIND, AND
HEART INVOLVEMENT IN EVERY MOMENT.

Within the astral and the physical planes are beings who have not yet realized their freedom from the wheel of karma or involuntary reincarnation. Discarnate beings are often attracted to certain incarnate beings who have the same desires and feelings. There is no need to fear discarnate entities any more than there is a need to fear incarnate personalities. All beings come to us within the physical and the non-physical worlds for a reason. Either we are attracted to one another by similar thoughts, feelings, and interests, or one is attracted to us because they need help and want to be freed from some level of bondage. I have encountered discarnate beings who simply want to be released into the Light. They are usually feeling afraid, confused, and disconnected. There are entities within both the third and the fourth dimensions who are *crying* to be released from the ignorance and pain of their separated state.

I am told that there are also entities who delight in deceiving the innocent because it fulfills their desire to control. It is my guess that these entities are attracted to incarnate beings who are also interested in controlling others for their own personal gain. These entities live on the lower astral plane because they are still attracted to the duality play. These so-called *dark forces* like to maintain their dominion over Earth-bound souls. They are often clever in knowing how to get one's attention and energy. However, the only way that the dark forces can really find an inroad is through the lower aspects of one's own ego. They are drawn to those who desire to have control over others, and they are also attracted to leaders who want power for themselves.

In the metaphysical world, these so-called dark forces find those who are wide open and unfocused in their meditations. There they insinuate themselves as channeled entities who deceive the innocent with promises of spiritual advancement. These devious powers love to find those who have little or no true self-esteem, and they are equally fond of finding those who are not fully occupying their own bodies. In both cases, entities are given a mind and a body that may be receptive to their needs and desires. Here they can inflate the meditator's ego by saying that he or she was once a famous person who has now returned to the world in order to complete some great mission. This appeal to the ego is all done in the hopes of diverting one from discovering that real love, wisdom, and power come only from one's own I AM Presence.

Fortunately, guardian angels watch over us from birth. They work hand-in-hand with one's own body elemental, whose task it is to oversee the intelligence of one's physical body. However, we still have free will, so it is vitally important that you do not consciously give anyone, even an Ascended Master, dominion over your soul! Realize that your own God- Presence (through the Christ Flame within your heart) is the only one who should ever be in charge of your life. Be conscious of your divinity and your connection to Source at all times. If you find yourself being contacted by subtle plane entities, I would recommend that you call forth the Christ, the archangels, and their celestial host to take these discarnate beings into their own remembrance as individualized souls of God-Light and God-Love. This will let the entities know that they do not need *your* light to survive or to work out their unresolved karma. Just as you would remind the living that they are of the Light, here is your opportunity to remind the *dead* that they were also born of God. Your calls to the Greater Light can bring these entities into alignment with their own evolutionary paths. They will be very grateful for your intervention on their behalf.

Before true freedom is understood and earned, many souls must wait on some level of the astral plane (the fourth dimension) before finding the right set of circumstances and timing for their next incarnation. Here on Earth, or on some other third-dimensional planet,[25] they are once again given the opportunity to fulfill their desires and to receive the lessons that duality teaches. Often people want to come back to improve their romantic relationships, to become more skillfull at social interactions, to utilize their powers of creativity, to manifest power as wealth, or to increase compassion by serving humanity. It is my understanding that ultimate freedom

---

[25] When the Earth goes into the fifth dimension, other planets will continue to teach the lessons of third-dimensional life.

can only be realized through mastery in a physical plane world. Once we have created patterns of limited thought and feeling, or initiated relationships that remain unresolved on any dimension of being, then we are responsible for healing or cleansing that karma. For many of us, *now* is that time! The good news is that we are receiving a lot of grace and a lot of help from the Spiritual Hierarchy, and due to the significance of this cosmic moment, we are being freed from a great deal of unredeemed karma.

Mastering Polarity

Even when it is extremely painful,
most of humankind choose to stay within the known
and to follow the path of least resistance.

POLARITY MAY BE DEFINED as any tendency to turn, grow, think, or feel in a certain way because of magnetic attraction or repulsion. Polarity involves the having or showing of any two *contrary* qualities or powers. By living on the Earth and by having physical-emotional bodies, we are constantly being affected by the magnetic forcefields that surround and penetrate our third and fourth-dimensional worlds. The play between the dark and the light forces has existed for millenniums as a strengthening game. It *only* takes place, as far as I know, within the third and fourth dimensions. However, if we don't understand how to rise above the game, we will be constantly victimized by the subliminal suggestions of the media and the fear-filled, limiting thought projections of the mass consciousness.

We can only live in Christ Consciousness by choosing a new reality and by creating new paradigms based on equality within the Law of the One (the Law of Love). We will need to monitor our thoughts and actions until we know that we have made a permanent shift into fifth-dimensional consciousness. This sounds like an awesome responsibility, but self-mastery has always invited us to meet the challenges of mindfulness.

Within a physical incarnation, there seems to be a tremendous mental and emotional pull to become a part of the drama that is continually taking place between all kinds of opposing forces. Mastery is achieved by the individual who learns how to witness the play between polarities and yet remains centered in the heart and unattached to either side. This central place of power would not *eliminate* polarity or even healthy competition. It would, however, place them both into a much more appropriate perspective.

When we come to realize that our self-worth is not dependent on winning or losing, on being male or female, on being right or wrong or even on being physical or spiritual beings, then we will be better able to enjoy the polarity play that exists within a third-dimensional world. When polarity and competition are viewed and enjoyed from a perspective of non-attachment, then we can simply utilize the power of their inherent energies as just a small part of the great creative process.

The emotional body pulses in resonance with where you *live* in your mind. As mentioned in the preceding chapters, your emotional and mental bodies are always projecting thoughtforms into your aura and into your immediate environment. If your emotional body is reflecting a discordant state of mind, then often the people around you will begin exhibiting the same or similar energies. We, as a race, have a tendency to match and merge with each others vibrational fields unless we learn how to live from a place of sovereignty as Christ-conscious, multidimensional beings.

The new fifth-dimensional paradigm, which is sustaining the Christ Consciousness grid around our planet, is teaching us not only how to live as heart-centered sovereign beings, but also how to serve the heart of humanity in its relationship to the Spiritual Hierarchy, the planet, the galaxy and the universe. Heart Initiates are beginning to understand the true value and importance of sustaining the Christ vibration under all circumstances. Some are learning how to commune as pure energy beings who just happen to be living in physical bodies. We have waited for this spiritual *communion* for thousands of years.

It is a tremendous awakening to see, feel, and know that you really do create and live within your own reality. When I finally came to terms with this, I had another immediate realization: no one *shares* my reality! This was the difficult part. I think we all really want to find at least one other person who is really living in *our* world. I have since found a place which can be shared; it is the place of the heart. It is the center between polarities, and although the world of the mind may always be individualized according to differences in schooling, home life, metaphysical training, spiritual upbringing, etc., the frequency of love remains the one constant in a ever changing world. God, as Love, cannot really be defined, but when you are one with It, you know it. It is the place of pure consciousness within the core of your soul, that place where you no longer feel alone or separate even though you are still living in a world where there are as many diverse realities as there are points of awareness to experience them.

As human beings living on a watery planet, we are often unconsciously pushed and pulled by the natural polarities that exist within nature, such as the cycles of the moon and the seasons of the year. Movement and rhythm are constant in a physical world. My emotions and body seem to work together as a unit of consciousness when they want to respond to the natural activities of the planet. As I become more sensitive, I am actually responding more and more to the pulsations that exist within all of life. On the freeway today, for example, my husband called my attention to a man on a motorcycle who was really driving dangerously. He was playing *cat-and-mouse* with a sports car and, as I watched, I began to lose my entire sense of equilibrium and well-being.

It is becoming increasingly easy for me to merge with the energies of whatever I am observing, and that is the risk of living in Unity Consciousness (where the observer and the observed become one). **The only thing that I seem to be able to do under these**

kinds of circumstances is to shift my focus to the realms of illumined truth where the eternal, unconditional mind can lift the temporal, conditional mind out of its fear-based reactivity to the unknown. In order to master polarity, I am slowly learning how to perceive everything and everyone on a purely energetic level. This is becoming incredibly freeing!

By viewing everything and everyone (including myself) as energy, vibration, and consciousness, I am noticing that my pain and my pleasure are totally determined by the choices I make in every living moment. Attachments to any level of conditional reality, even those involving other people, come from these choices. When I discipline myself to see, hear, and respond to what is occuring outside of memories or future projections, I am able to eliminate the need to deal with past or future fears. This leaves me free to *act*, rather than to *react*, to what has been or what might be tomorrow.

From choices that we have made about life during our major turning points, generally associated with trauma, we often repeat life patterns that are no longer serving us. Like dams in a mighty river, negative patterning can cause one's energy to become blocked, diverted, or drained. Most people have not even begun to live as free-spirited human beings. For the duration of an entire lifetime, one can remain separated and blocked from receiving the full current of God's Love and Power through the physical and emotional bodies. When we are disassociated from the Heart of the True Self, we are really unable to see and embrace the living splendor of God in others.

The energy contained within our self-negating thoughts is tremendous. We can, however, completely redirect ALL of this so-called negative energy so that it can be used for our highest personal and planetary good. Please know that it is only the "lunar" or reflective facets of the emotional self that are attracted and attached to being right or wrong, high or low, happy or sad. By not identifying with these polarized extremes of the human character and yet fully embracing their play in your life, you will be able to remain within the center point of your power. By embracing the *unlovable* aspects of yourself and simply seeing them as reservoirs of untapped creative energy, you will experience more joy and enthusiasm in your ongoing transformation.

To take this next leap, you need to birth yourself out of self-judgment by knowing that you can feel and experience all your thoughts and feelings without any great conflict or admonishment from your inner critic. Although the majority of humankind continue to drain themselves by repeating unsupportive patterns, they often do not really know how to change. If there is *only* energy, vibration, and consciousness, then we each have the God-given dominion to direct energy by focusing light and love on what we really want to create!

The following visualization may assist you in entering into your heart as your central focus of power. To augment your concentration, please place yourself in a quiet environment where you will not be disturbed. Breathe rhythmically for a few moments while placing your full attention in your heart. You may want to call in your I AM Presence, the Christ, the Ascended Masters, or whomever you feel is appropriate for this meditation. It is always empowering to do an opening prayer.

VISUALIZATION EXERCISES FOR
USING THE FORCES OF POLARITY

To do this exercise, you will be creating three figure-eights in your mind's eye. Please do them sequentially, as they are described below. Visualize the center point of each figure-eight crossing through your body at the heart. Allow yourself to feel the liquid light motion of all three of these figure-eights as they flow through your heart center. You may want to do this exercise while you are *standing* within an imaginary tube of brilliant light.

a. See the first "eight" going up and down, or vertically. Ask that it harmonize the multidimensional levels of your Self, also referred to as your Lightbodies, with your physical body. Allow this figure-eight to go all the way to the Great Central Sun (or to Source) and into the Earth's central core. This will establish your full momentum as a spiritual, physical, and planetary being.

b. See the second "eight" going backward and forward while allowing it to harmonize your past and future lives with the power of the present time moment in which you are living. Here you are collecting and dissolving the projections of your past and future images or identities, both real and imagined. You are bringing all of your ideas about your human self into the heart of your Christ-self.

c. See the third "eight" going side to side, or horizontally, while it balances your inner male and female within the left and right sides of your brain and body. Here you are healing within your Heart Flame all the extremes that may still be at war between your inner man and woman, or your mental and feeling natures. These polarized aspects of the Self can hereby be freed to merge in your heart as one indivisible force of Love and Light, allowing the true wisdom of the inner Christ to come forward.

AN ALTERNATIVE VISUALIZATION WOULD INVOLVE ALIGNING YOUR HEART WITH THE POWER OF THE SEVEN DIRECTIONS: THE NORTH, THE SOUTH, THE EAST, THE WEST, ABOVE, BELOW, AND CENTER. THIS IS KNOWN AS THE "GALACTIC MEDICINE WHEEL."

a. Place the center of a vertical figure-eight in your heart, and run the circular fields of the "eight" up into the galactic center (or Central Sun of our galaxy), as well as down into the core of the Earth. (This embraces the ABOVE, BELOW, and CENTER aspects of your medicine wheel.)

b. Keeping the center at your heart, now run a horizontal figure-eight from the left to the right of your body. Align the right arm of your "eight" with the visionary powers of the EAST, and the left arm of your "eight" with the transformational powers of the WEST.

c. Now run another horizontal figure-eight from front to back, while again centering it at your heart. Align the front arm with the NORTH, or the wisdom functions of the adult self, and the back arm with the SOUTH, or the innocent qualities of the inner child.

WHEN ONE'S ENERGY POTENTIAL IS UNDERSTOOD, THEN ONE CAN USE POLARITY FROM A PLACE OF POWER.

During these often difficult times, it is important to remember that we are all finding ways to release the pent-up emotions of our sad, angry, lonely, and often wounded inner selves. As we proceed to master our abilities to unconditionally embrace what is happening, we can no longer remain the victim of the world, of another, or of our own past. Many of you are the pioneers who have chosen to dive into your transformational processes without a road map or a role model. Everyone has a part to play, whether they are quiet participants, active flag wavers, or blessed supporters of those who are more publicly engaged.

Many Lightworkers are behind the scenes, emotionally and mentally freeing themselves from present and past life patterning. They are to be applauded for their dedication in transmuting their unnecessary patterning. There comes a time, however, when the inner healing reaches such a stage of completion that they feel safe enough and strong enough to start living their greater destiny as masterful beings. As free and empowered Initiates of the Heart, many of these dedicated individuals are now reentering the world as very capable Lightworkers.

YOU are an integral part of actualizing "Thy Will be done on Earth as it is in heaven!" *You are the Word being made flesh!* You are here to actualize what it means *to be of the world and not in it.* Although it is imperative that you take yourself out of denial by releasing and healing your past, it is equally important to focus on who you are as God's Love and God's Light, and to remain clear on how you want to individualize your Self and your service in the world.

The lower mind lives in resonance with the separative tendencies of the ego. It is anchored in fear for its own survival. Now we are finding that there is another mind, a mind which is *not* dualistic and which is not intent on remaining separate. This "higher mind" is based instead on the principles of unification with all life. There really is a time when we can and do *round the bend* in our healing processes, and it is then that we begin to experience the harmony of living as truly sovereign beings.

We, as a race, are a continuing experiment in free will. You must decide whether or not you are willing to see, to understand, to heal, and to love free any remaining emotional wounds or mental patterning that may be hidden within the confines of your memory fields or within those of your family tree. You can only love yourself free by acknowledging all aspects of your human experience. So-called negative energies can then be transmuted and redirected.

Since polarity is a part of life on the third and fourth dimensions, we are still using opposites to create our realities. By always looking for the lessons within what *appears* to be a negative thought, feeling, or situation, you can find the hidden power that even the most difficult challenges contain. By conscious volition, you can choose to shift your attention to the opposite side of the energy coin when you feel it is appropriate. It is important that you do not abort your feelings in this process.

NEW PERSPECTIVES ON POLARITY

THE PAST

Sorrow releases. It breaks the tension, clears the air, and connects us to the core of our vulnerability. Most people do not want to lose the walls of protection that the ego-body-mind has created to remain safe. The ego struggles to remain free of pain. To surrender to the suffering seems to take away what is stable, creating fear within the psyche. Surrendering to God is also surrendering to the fear and pain inside. This initially appears to weaken one, but in fact it strengthens that which is real and kills that which is false. When deep sadness is combined with remorse and fear of loss, it keeps us from seeing that vulnerability can be positive.

As we ascend, all energy becomes positive. The trials of the past imprison our hearts until we break through to the underlying suffering, which ironically has the power to birth us into higher levels of feeling. When we empty ourselves, we make room for the Holy Spirit to enter our bodies, and our hearts fill with compassion for all life.

REMORSE INVALIDATES (THE SELF);
GRATITUDE VALIDATES.

THE PRESENT

Anger is frequently repressed in our society. If anger remains unexpressed or unacknowledged for too long a time, then we often avoid releasing it for fear of being destructive. Anger can fester internally unless it is consciously expressed or transmuted. It is often born out of the belief that we do not have enough power to protect ourselves, our boundaries, or our integrity. Anger gives us the intense energy that we think we need in order to control others. Anger is similar to fear in that it affects our glandular system. Unattended anger inhibits your mastery of the present, as it binds you to the survival instincts of your primal self.

Please note that responsible anger can be transmuted into useful assertive energy for outlining your desires without undue conflict or damage to another. The so-called negative emotions, such as anger and fear, often contain the energetic propulsion that we sometimes need to get things done and said. Do not feel guilty for having these intense emotions, but rather use them for everyone's benefit.

GUILT INVALIDATES (THE SELF);
JOY VALIDATES.

THE FUTURE

The aura has instinctual *feelers* that alert us when trouble is near. Fear warns our glandular system, which responds by secreting hormones that give us the extra energy that we need in order to survive. These kind of instinctive reactions also take place when our egos are threatened. You can verify this by paying attention to the feelings you have in your solar plexus the next time you feel you are losing control. Fear causes tightening; absence of fear feels relaxed or expanded.

The energy of fear can be transformed into courage, thus creating an excitement in the heart that can strengthen your power to remain centered. Fear can, therefore, be transmuted into the kind of enthusiasm that supports your willingness to be the Self.

FEAR INVALIDATES (THE SELF);
ENTHUSIASM VALIDATES.

Earth Shift

And he carried me away in the spirit to a great and high mountain, and showed me that great city, the holy Jerusalem, descending out of heaven from God.

— Revelation 21:10,
Holy Bible, Lamsa translation

IN HER BOOK, *We, The Arcturians,* Dr. Norma Milanovich states that the Earth is being consumed by the Great Central Sun, and that this is already occurring at an incredibly rapid speed. Scientists report that our galaxy is being magnetically pulled through the heavens at an amazing speed toward what they are calling the Great Attractor. Both of these postulations indicate that the Earth is moving, or being moved, into a place in the universe that is going to provide it with a new *heavenly* home. Dr. Milanovich goes on to say that when the Earth does indeed move into her new atmosphere, the inhabitants of the planet will be supported by the energy, vibration, and consciousness of the fifth dimension, which will be its new culture.

We are in a temporary and necessary transformational adjustment period. The third and fourth dimensions are still with us, only we are learning how to relate to their lessons while using more of a fifth-dimensional perspective. You will develop increasing faith and confidence as you adjust to operating from the heart of this *new* dimensional reality. You will also find that you are not alone. Both those on the Earth and those off of the Earth are here to support you in making this great shift. Many unseen guardians are assisting us during this major shift, partly because they are also being affected by our changes and partly because they are our appointed overseers and educators, having already made the transition themselves.

You are moving as a *whole being* into increasingly higher octaves of consciousness. The people and circumstances which come into your life on the third dimension are often very significant. Your spiritual overseers are placing you in contact with specific others in order that greater service can be accomplished. This could even mean that you need to accomplish important spiritual work with the members of your own family! Often Lightworkers feel that their family relationships are hopeless. When this is actually the case, then families provide one with the gift of learning how to move into sovereignty without receiving or needing their support. Treading the path alone often provides one with an even greater sense of the Self than is derived from being protected within the family matrix. Relatives, however, can be tremendously valuable allies. We need to discern what adds to our evolvement and what detracts from it.

We incarnate into our families for many reasons. There is often a great love bonding that is never seen until we are willing to dive deep into the mirrors that our family members provide. If family members want to make the shift into the fifth dimension together, then they need to care enough about each other to understand, forgive, and love free their mutually accumulated karma. It is probably very rare to find a family where all members are spiritually working toward the same goals. In any case, it is always beneficial to do some visualization exercises,[26] and to get some professional assistance for releasing all of the inherited physical, emotional, and mental patterning that is no longer serving you or your path.

Although we sometimes find friends who seem to be closer to us than our own family members, I cannot overemphasize the

---

[26] *Soul Alignment*, an audio tape by Julianne Everett, addresses this kind of release work. It may be ordered from the publisher.

importance of clearing any outstanding family karma at this time in our collective evolution. If you are the most spiritually conscious member of your family, then you are probably the one to start the healing process. I guarantee you that any effort you make to bring your family unit into more love will greatly free your heart.

When the denser energies that support separation and duality are released within our homes, our hearts, and our bodies, then the new personal and planetary ascension templates can set the transfiguration part of the Christ Process into high gear. The body then begins shifting and lifting into the higher dimensional frequencies, often causing physical and emotional side effects. When you first begin entering the fifth-dimensional consciousness grid, you may feel extremely vulnerable, slightly disoriented, physically unstable, very lightheaded, and overwhelmingly loving. You may also feel afraid, unsafe, and incapable of functioning on the third dimension with mental clarity, emotional stability, and physical strength. The very thought of completely shifting your third-dimensional mind and body into a new dimensional frequency may seem, at times, overwhelming. The good news is that your child-like innocence and vulnerability is a good indication that you are already on your surfboard, riding the wave into the new.

As the accrued energies of the past are being increasingly neutralized, you may find that you are becoming forgetful. This forgetfulness will pass when you get more used to living from the Christ Flame within your heart. For it is there that your I AM Presence will take charge of your being and teach you how to operate from wisdom rather than from accumulated knowledge and past information. At first you may not trust yourself to get things accomplished on the third dimension. Surrendering to the Presence in the power of every moment takes courage.

If you experience light-headedness, just know that this feeling often comes from having less dross in your aura and body. This is often a good indication that you are really transmuting your cells into light. On the down side, however, this could also mean that you are mentally and spiritually leaving your body. As my transformation progresses, there are times that an inexplicable fear rushes to the surface, forcing me to either be more present or to escape by leaving the body. If this happens to you, try taking deep breaths, down into your abdomen, while you imagine your energies moving into the bottom of your feet with each breath.

THE GREATEST CHALLENGE
THAT YOU WILL EVER ENCOUNTER
IS YOURSELF.

Just realizing this will assist you in overcoming the hold that your ego-body-mind may have in getting you to believe that you must remain separate and bound to the third or fourth dimensions. The idea of *Oneness,* or fifth-dimensional consciousness, is the most frightening prospect that the ego can encounter. If you inform the ego and the survival mechanisms that it has placed into your lower chakras that it is time for *all of you* to be lifted into a new dimensional frequency, then there will be less of a battle, or perhaps none at all. Place your intention on lifting your ego into the new so that it can *serve* your higher consciousness, rather than *fight* with it. This will certainly make the journey more pleasant.

You can assist the Ascended Masters in shifting your lower self into the fifth dimension by agreeing to take time to meditate. To live in freedom, one's primary commitment must be to establishing a relationship with God. Ask your Higher Self what you can do to increase your ability to commune in the Oneness with your I AM Presence. Meditation can be both active or passive. Although it is always created out of the silence, it can involve communication with your Higher Self and/or your spiritual guides. Your teachers often use meditation as an opportunity to assist you in focusing on some aspect of your internal journey, or they may want to direct your attention towards some facet of your external service.

True mediation will always carry you deeper into Love and Light, keep you completely centered at the heart, and consume you totally in the power of the moment. True meditation is completely filled with the essence of the Holy Spirit because it is outside of time-bound awareness. This embodiment is providing us all with an opportunity for learning how to actually act, think, feel, and speak from the meditative state.

We are being activated and awakened to more consciously align with our destiny within the greater Universe. Earth emissaries[27] are being invited to participate with the Solar, Galactic, and Universal Councils of Light. Many *Starseeds* are here to assist us in understanding what this really means. These beings are now awakening to their true heritage. They are realizing why they have come here and how they want to serve. Many are already living in the consciousness of the fifth, sixth, and seventh dimensions. These Starseeds carry the encodings that we often need to see, hear, and feel before we are truly willing to shift our lower bodies into their higher-dimensional frequencies.

The heart chakra is aligning us with the frequency wave band of Unity Consciousness on the fifth dimension so that the lower bodies can ascend. However, the throat, brow, and crown chakras are actually being aligned with the sixth, seventh, and eighth dimensions! We are being given a glorious opportunity to rise out of our collective amnesia and separation from the greater universe so that we may consciously create with beings from other dimensions who *already* live in multidimensional states of consciousness while in ongoing service to the One.

"Each planet and star system goes through similar periods of trials and errors as the Earth is doing right now. We are here to help one of the most difficult birthing processes that has ever been the challenge to

---

27 Those who have elected to serve the Planetary Logos by consciously acting as liaisons for the Earth within the Solar, Galactic, and Universal Councils of the Cosmic Christ Light. These Councils are extended branches of the One Spiritual Hierarchy.

any of the beings in the universe. The moment for the quantum leap into the future is nearing the critical mass point, and we are hoping that the delay will not cause a retardation period for the beloved Terra. We are here primarily to highlight the spiritual path for Earthlings and to protect the children of Light. We are here to work with all to ensure that the beloved Terra will achieve her destiny.

"Earthlings have a tendency to resist change and the new, and do not generally wish to progress into unknown realities and the beauty of other dimensions. The people of Earth are on a path that is irreversible. On this journey they must realize that Light and Love are the only two qualities that can be adhered to for advancement into the New Age. We are not speaking of the moment of time to accomplish this that is equivalent to a small day, month, or even a year. We are talking about a transit of time, over the next several years, that will transform the energy of the beloved Earth to a Garden of Eden in the galaxy."[28]

One primary function which we can each perform in order to make this magnificent dimensional shift a little smoother is to seriously monitor our thoughts and completely alter the way in which we perceive and create our realities. We can remove our attention from the *negative* by seeing it differently. By taking responsibility for all areas of thought, word, emotion, and activity which promote separation, we can become responsible co-creators who have the dominion to remove all that is hampering or blocking us from our full potential as free and conscious human beings.

CONSTANTLY FOCUS ON WHAT YOU
REALLY WANT TO MANIFEST!
DO NOT PROTECT OR NOURISH THAT WHICH IS
UNWORTHY OF YOUR SACRED ATTENTION.

---

[28] *We, The Arcturians* by Dr. Norma Milanovich

All energy is God's! As emissaries of God's Love and Light, we have been given the free will to qualify or to requalify this sacred energy with our thoughts and feelings. If we really desire to create a new planetary consciousness, then we must often shift the way in which we perceive ourselves, our life, and our world. For example, all inharmonious situations can be viewed with a sense of excitement! Feed your co-creative juices by seeing the power, the love, and the wisdom that lies dormant within the seed of every area of conflict or disharmony. Any fragment of life which supports limitation, separation, or negativity also contains the great potential for transmutation. Remember how much you wanted to be here to help in making this shift the most awesome event in human history.

Soul Contracts

"And let us not grow weary while doing good, for in due season we shall reap if we do not lose heart."

— Galatians 6:9

Every star and planet extends to us an opportunity for mastering ever new and higher levels of consciousness. All planetary bodies exist in accordance with certain universal laws that appear to keep them in celestial attunement with their Source. There seems to be no confusion in the higher worlds. Cosmic states of consciousness are determined by how well we resonate with these higher laws and with the lighter, more expanded frequencies of the unlimited Self. Divine Intelligence plays no favorites. Your mastery is simply determined by where you are living in your consciousness.

We do not know, nor can we afford to assume, what the next step is for anyone. We cannot see from our limited perspectives that one field of accomplishment is higher or lower than another. All of these factors are determined by one's destiny for balancing and birthing the soul into a greater and greater expression of the Self. Each soul brings lifetimes of collective wisdom into every incarnation. Through all the centuries of being, either in embodiment or in our subtle Lightbodies between incarnations, we have been expanding our capacities to live and love from the unlimited Heart and Mind of God.

We must actually *ascend* in consciousness in order to begin to live in the Oneness that exists in the higher dimensions, beginning with the fifth dimension. Christians tells us that we need to pray to our "Father Who Art in Heaven" and to accept Jesus the Christ as our Lord and Savior. This is their interpretation of how we can bring the Christ energy into our hearts and thereby live in a constant state of Oneness with God. It is important that we realize *heaven* as a state of consciousness, wherein we can live in true union with God while we are here *on Earth*.

The desire to leave the Earth and to ascend into some heavenly world is a driving force within many religious seekers. Some Eastern religions tell us that we can become God-realized while living here on Earth. Eastern adepts are sometimes able to enter into *samadhi* or *nirvana* where they do experience conscious union with God. These states of realization are sustained by going into such deep levels of meditation that one basically becomes non-functional on the physical plane.

In this century, many Eastern adepts have reincarnated into the Western world. These masters are used to living in solitude. Now they are being challenged to bring the great peace of their conscious nirvanic states of God-union into their lives and worlds while living among the people. They are being asked to live as conscious spiritual wayshowers because they have prepared themselves for centuries to assist the Spiritual Hierarchy in bringing Christ Consciousness into the world.

Many of you who are reading this book have experienced God-union by entering into what is called the "cave of Brahma" in the pineal gland. This gland is associated with the crown chakra and its activation does indeed bring one into a state of enlightenment, or total union with God's Love and Light. The material world, however, does not support living in nirvana. Unless you are living in isolation, it is difficult to sustain this perfect state of divine union.

IN THIS INCARNATION WE ARE FACING THE GREAT CHALLENGE OF LIVING AS ENLIGHTENED BEINGS IN PHYSICAL BODIES IN A PHYSICAL WORLD!

Groups are coming together to remind one another of our great assignment: to bring the already enlightened I AM Presence, centered in the crown chakra, down into the heart chakra, where Love can take over the body and send it out into the world to heal the separation. This Light of *All That Is* must also be taken into the lower body until every cell becomes God-realized and we know that we are truly home.

Our liberation from the Earth plane will most probably come when our souls have truly consummated the service for which we originally came. Very few people are actually conscious of why they are here or of what soul contracts they made before birth. In her book, *Embraced By The Light,* Betty Eadie shares with us that those who have temporarily passed over in near-death experiences come back into this world in order to complete their soul contracts. Many of these *returnees* tell us that we only come here to learn how to love more unconditionally and that everything on the inner planes exists in *fields* of pure Love and Light.

Sometimes our Earth contracts involve many levels of karma, which the soul can only complete while living in the physical world. So often, people think of karma as difficult or painful. However, this planet also provides us with an opportunity to experience positive karma, especially in the area of relationships. In either case, become aware of the tremendous sense of fulfillment and relief that can come from releasing the past and the parts that you played in its creation. Love is the common thread, the only constant that holds us together while we play out our parts and learn our lessons in these precious bodies that express so perfectly the miracle of God's Love.

 The New Feeling Body

" ... They shall obtain joy and gladness, and sorrow and sighing shall flee away."

— Isaiah 35:10

COMPASSION IS THE SISTER OF PASSION. Passion holds and then releases the energies for creating in the manifest world. Compassion contains the fire of love's desire to care about others. Both of these feelings activate the liquid light which carries the life-force through our bodies and into the world. Conscious alignment between our feeling nature and our spiritual Lightbodies is being reestablished during these times. This may sound like a ho-hum statement, but we have been waiting for centuries to ascend into our greater capacities to give and receive love. It is truly a most glorious cosmic event!

Just as we have been using only a small percentage of our brains, we have also been feeling only a fraction of our emotions. The opportunity that we now have for expanding into our higher love nature is one of the major reasons that so many souls are desiring to come to Earth during this cycle of our evolution. It is time for the feminine to awaken within every heart.

This planet has everything to offer the true Initiate of the Heart. Cosmic law seals our higher chakras until the heart is opened. In this way we are not given authentic spiritual power prematurely. The Heart Flame of the Christ-self expresses and balances its three-fold nature of Love, Wisdom, and Power. Mastering this triadic integration is the challenge of every Initiate. It is the way out of duality. *It is the master key to one's ascension.*

WE ARE FREEING OURSELVES FROM THE CODINGS
WHICH HAVE BOUND US INTO BELIEVING
THAT WE ARE MORTAL BEINGS
WHO MUST EXIST IN COMPETITION AND SURVIVAL.

We no longer need to compare our gifts, our services, our bodies, or our minds with any other human being. Release from the fear of not being good enough or of being less than someone else brings a tremendous sense of internal and external relief. The Ascended Masters greatly applaud this giant step upward from the competitiveness of the solar plexus to the unconditional love of the heart — from the sword to the word, from the warrior to the lover. Though we bring forth the gifts we have brought with us from other incarnations, the Heart Flame must be reunited with and re-activated by the Holy Spirit before true freedom is realized. It is not that one must throw away the good life to live the God Life, but we do need to understand what the "good life" really is!

What is a true marriage or relationship? What is real communication? How does polarity relate to duality? Is your passion balanced with compassion? Is your assertive nature coming from knowing who you are, or is it arising from a position of inferiority or help-lessness? Are you coming from contraction or expansion? The bottom line: is your life love-based or fear-based?

The major discipline of my life has been to consistently practice living from the truth of my feelings, while remaining centered in my heart. There are signposts which continually assist me in learning where my feelings originate. Do I feel overly impatient, attached to the outcome, unable to listen to another's viewpoint, or afraid that I may not be heard or understood? All of these emotions would indicate that I still need to understand and heal the reactivity of my lower self. Were I coming from my heart, I would be able to freely listen to another's viewpoint, I would not be attached to being heard or even understood, and I would most probably see the "other side" of the situation with a clear mind *and* a relaxed solar plexus.

Please understand that this does NOT mean you must roll over and play dead. This also does NOT mean that you must feel guilty or judgmental about your emotional reactivity. Just because you align with and center yourself in the witness position of your Higher Self and you develop understanding and compassion for other people's viewpoints, does not mean you are required to give up saying or doing what you feel is right or appropriate!

I used to be very adept at giving in *and* giving up, feeling that this was the humanitarian thing to do. I would quietly slide into oblivion at every sign of conflict. This was not empowering to me or to others. I completely misunderstood the deeper meaning behind true spiritual surrender. When real heart communication takes place, everyone is left feeling empowered and good about themselves.

THE MOST EFFECTIVE AND CREATIVE COMMUNICATION MOST OFTEN COMES THROUGH THOSE WHO ARE CONNECTED TO THEIR DEEP AND TRUE FEELINGS.

Everything stems from living your truth. This may or may not have anything to do with trying to make others happy. The significant others in your life are really the happiest when you are happy. This is true unless you, your friends, your families, or your mates are being deceived by the veils of co-dependency. For so many years and so many lifetimes we have needed each other for support and to assuage the various wounds that have accumulated in the physical, mental, emotional, and etheric bodies. The wounded child develops all kinds of defensive attitudes in order to protect itself from feeling pain.

It is all right to need each other. One of the reasons we come to Earth is to learn *how* to love and how to give real emotional support when and where we can. If we gossip in non-constructive ways or insist on projecting negative, limiting thoughts onto other people and their way of life, then we are adding to their suffering and our own. Failure, sorrow, anger, fear, and pain have been a big part of life on this planet for a long, long time. We are probably not going to avoid some kind of suffering if we have decided to be fully alive to our feelings. Lasting joy seems to be possible when we accept the whole package deal. I think that we, as a culture, have had an unreal idea of what happiness is.

> *THE SEARCH FOR GOD IS RELATED TO*
> *THE SEARCH FOR ONE'S SELF.*
> *GOD WANTS US TO LIVE IN THE KIND OF JOY*
> *THAT COMES FROM JUST BEING OURSELVES!*

Outside stimulus only brings us temporary satisfaction, and that outside stimulus also includes the belief that we must experience union with an *external* God. When we are truly reunited with our *whole self*, we will quite naturally be reunited with God. The love, the wisdom, and the power we each have sought externally through so many varied lives and through so many diverse experiences, are all to be found within the heart. The *voice* of the heart has been stifled under a barrage of shame, guilt, anger, fear, envy, doubt, and sorrow. It is difficult to hear the still, small voice of a buried and shielded heart!

Our internal and our external heart connections are meant to become ever clearer and stronger. At times, it seems that we are disconnected from ourselves and from each other. These are the days that we feel lost and lonely. The good news is that you know, you truly and deeply know, that *real* love can never be taken away or permanently lost. Your heart sustains your pure God-essence, and in that you are permanently connected to your beloved twin ray,[29] whether he or she is with you on the physical plane or not.

---

[29] Twin Ray is the counterpart of one's soul. The Ascended Master teachings state that we split into two parts when coming to this planet.

You and your twin ray are always one within the higher consciousness of your I AM Presence. When you are awakened within your
seventh-dimensional consciousness, which is where your Presence
abides, then your connection with the twin ray will become so
natural that it may even go unnoticed.

Every person has only one twin ray. There are many companions of the soul, however, who are commonly called soulmates.
Some soulmates find each other to complete unfinished karma;
some come together to serve the planet; and some are drawn
together to simply keep the love going. Every soulmate who comes
into your life is giving you a glorious opportunity to physically and
emotionally practice unconditional love. If you have experienced
the living essence of those who make up the many Councils of Light
within the Spiritual Hierarchy, then you know how we each need
to practice unconditional love!

As multidimensional beings, it is important for us to remember
that our Higher Selves are *always* living in these pure states of
Oneness with all of Life. More than ever before, we can now assist
each other in *remembering* the kind of divine love that naturally
supports Unity Consciousness. Remembering is a tremendous gift
of Grace being given to ease our fears so that we will surrender
more easily to the Holy Spirit. **The complete mental and
emotional willingness to *surrender* to God as Love can tremendously escalate an Initiate's progress toward Christ
Consciousness.**

As we enter our new consciousness light zone, we are going to
start experiencing cosmic union within ourselves and within our
planetary relationships. We are now on the outskirts of that zone
and there are already reports of people experiencing what could be
termed *full-body cosmic orgasms*. These "orgasms" do not involve
erections or ejaculations, in either males or females, but they do
involve what feels like a full-body cellular release that eventually
fountains out of the top of the head, followed by a concurrent rush
downward leaving one in an ecstatic state of renewal and divine

love. This light zone, which is also being called the Photon Belt, is actually lifting the consciousness of our cells back into divine reunion with Source. We are literally being attracted by the great Love magnet of the Creator.

The Transfiguration is at hand — our material cells are transforming into Light cells! Within the creative force of absolute Love all possibilities exist! When we have enough faith to surrender our separateness, then we allow the love, the light, the sound, and the color of the higher-dimensional frequencies to come in and transform our lives on every level of the Self. Although I have experienced cosmic union on several occasions, I cannot really *make* it happen. As the I AM Presence comes deeper into the Christ Flame of the heart, I suspect that cosmic union will become less orgasmic or will have less of a sensational effect within the body.

Most individuals know that they are alive because of their reactivity to circumstances or to another's actions. As we enter the new feeling body of the Christ Self, this will no longer be necessary. At first your life may even seem a little boring, until you discover that your new feelings are based on your power to act from the dominion of your heart. Many people have no idea of what it is to live from the authentic power of a cleared solar plexus and a fully awakened heart. They have instead been operating from an eclipsed position, or a *lunar plexus*, where power is only brought forth in relationship to someone else or to some outside set of circumstances.

Within the framework of your primary relationships, you can empower yourself and others by creating a deep commitment to reach for the highest love possible. Relationships are the playground that we have created for seeing how we are doing in giving and receiving love. It is within our ongoing relationships that we can practice living in the consciousness of the higher dimensions. Even the lessons of war can be used to transmute hate into love. No matter how horrendous the outer appearances may appear, we are always being given a chance to learn and to relearn the lessons of love. There is no real freedom until these lessons are taken to heart.

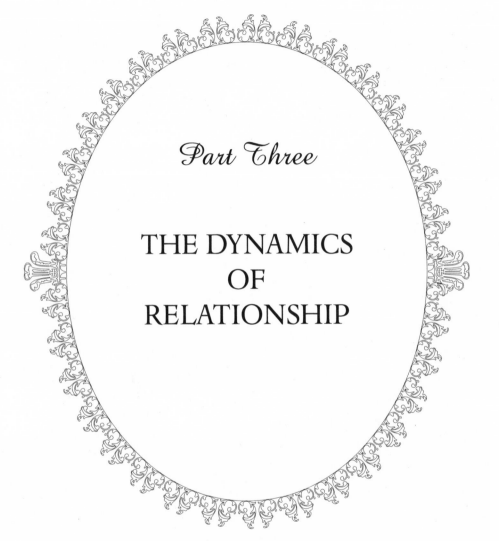

Part Three

THE DYNAMICS
OF
RELATIONSHIP

Sexual Liberation

"There is no fear in love ..."

— 1 John 4:18

SEXUAL UNION AND TOUCHING fulfill our needs to experience physical closeness. Loving partnerships seem to help us to feel worthwhile, but do they satisfy our deeper needs for self-intimacy and spiritual union? In our society, we have traditionally expected our mates to fulfill our dreams. If we believe that someone else is responsible for making us happy, then we project that expectation onto our partner. He or she may greatly resent that intrusion unless we are willing to openly discuss our desires and requests.

The new relationship paradigm requests that we have no hidden agendas. It is vitally important that we remain psychically clear of invading our partner's aura with *unspoken* thoughts, feelings, and expectations. Since most of us are not free enough to be without desire, then we must at least put our wants out into the open. Without communication, a relationship deteriorates under a barrage of unspoken anger, disappointment, sorrow, and resentment until at last the love is gone.

THOSE WITH WHOM WE ARE INTIMATE
FEEL THE PRESSURE OF WHAT IS LEFT UNSAID,
EVEN IF THEY CANNOT ALWAYS INTERPRET
THE THOUGHTS BEHIND THEIR FEELINGS.

Sexual union has been a necessary step in our evolution. It has satisfied our desires and our genetic instincts to not only populate a planet but also to bring our loved ones back into embodiment. When sexual appetites are unbalanced, a person becomes obsessed with physical needs and desires that are often expressed through abuse on many different levels, from conscious control and intimidation to rape and murder. If you are the recipient of another's abuse, then you probably believe on a conscious or unconscious level that you are not a very valuable person.

THERE IS DEEPER SEXUAL SATISFACTION WHEN THERE IS DEEPER SELF-ACCEPTANCE.

We sometimes arrange to find others to hurt us, either emotionally or physically, if we feel that we need to be punished for some past action. In part, we are here to respond to each other's needs and to act out the roles that often lie hidden within the agenda of the unconscious. We karmically attract our abusers, even though it may seem impossible to believe. For example, if a feeling of *guilt* is deeply recorded within one's cellular memory, then that feeling eventually projects outward, alerting others that there is a need to be punished. The so-called abuser will eventually come forth to fulfill that need.

If we invalidate ourselves or our gifts, or refuse to love ourselves or others, then we alert our four lower bodies to begin the death process. The physical body often accommodates self-invalidation by creating some kind of cancer. The emotional body may respond by making one increasingly incapable of feeling good and positive about life and others, which often leads to ill health in the physical heart. The mental body responds to lack of love by making it more and more difficult for one to create joy and abundance in his or her life. Although the mental body is generally the one which holds on to the last threads of life, it will also eventually deteriorate if it is not nourished by love.

Some people just seem to have an intense inborn desire to keep nourishing their own life process. The life urge really comes in clearly when one makes a conscious choice to accept life on its own terms. Those who can accept the heart expansion that comes with pain and suffering seem to live as freer, more loving beings. I have found that even spiritually-oriented people like to avoid pain, and they often harbor a secret longing to leave the planet. To successfully and joyfully ascend, *every cell* of the body must be filled with acceptance for what is. The life urge can be integrated on a cellular level when we consciously choose to live out our lives as masterful *physical* beings, facing each opportunity with the wisdom of the heart.

We are culturally aching to release our suffering so that we can express and experience more unconditional love. In the new culture, our passions and sexual desires will only reflect our deepest and highest desires to live in Unity Consciousness at all times. As we harmonize the lower chakras with the upper chakras, our primal needs will become more divine and we will be inspired to simply love one another every chance that we get. Compassion will override fear, greed, jealousy, and unhealthy competition, no matter what abusive actions may have taken place in the past.

The Spiritual Hierarchy and the angels are quickening our hearts so that we can really begin to *feel* more physical and spiritual intimacy. We are being guided to find others who will help us to heal the separation. Two or more people do not generally occupy the same field of reality for more than a few moments at a time. When a shared reality does take place, it creates an ecstatic flow within the heart, mind, and body of all those involved. Group meditation and guided visualizations into the truth of the heart are just two of the ways that men and women are beginning to experience the advantages of coming together as the One Self.

We are now being challenged to retrain ourselves to be more loving, direct, clear, and pure in our communications. I have noticed that one of the greatest areas of conflict between men and women is in *how* they communicate with one another. Women have learned how to communicate from the left hemisphere of the brain so that they can remain in touch with their men and the world. They often sacrifice their greatest gifts in order to be loved. This has created confusion in both sexes. Most women have lost the ability to speak from their heart, thus depriving *both* sexes of the energies that come from real spiritual union. Women must keep their emotional body alive and alert to the root of their highest spiritual nature if they are to truly serve their partners. No matter how terrifying it may be for the woman or how threatening it may be to her mate, a man really wants his woman to keep living from her heart. He wants a woman who can remain deeply in touch with her feelings, whether he is conscious of this desire or not. And a woman wants a man who is responsive to *her* need for intimacy.

Both men and women generally try to avoid being with partners who seem to be emotionally out of control, unless that is what they need to regain balance and harmony within themselves. It helps to understand that we are presently undergoing such a dramatic purification that irrational behavior will probably come forward until stabilization is reached and both partners have dipped into the unconditional love and wisdom of the Higher Self.

Great and often painful upheavals are naturally a part of one's transformation. When clearing the deep suffering that is often stored in the lower self, please remember that it is often through embracing *hell* that we enter into *heaven*. This is another paradox. The soul, however, really knows that one must access and take responsibility for his or her most abhorrent feelings in order to eventually make room for the Divine. Bless your willingness to keep your vision clear while you are transmuting the old limiting ways of being together.

Women are by nature more connected to their feelings. They more easily link with the subtle and spiritual worlds. This can be demeaning to the male ego unless a man has been spiritually awakened enough to understand the importance of the role of women at this time in our history. The mental body of both men and women has been in control of the true feeling nature of the heart for many centuries. There are bound to be inner and outer conflicts as personal and planetary purification progresses. Without the willingness to explore the whole world of feelings, a relationship can quickly be reduced to control issues, and neither partner will be emotionally or physically satisfied.

Most of us learn quite early in life that certain kinds of manipulation bring rewards. We are now learning how to direct energies from the heart, where there is never a need to control. From the wisdom flame of the Christ-within, we will become fully capable of seeing when and if we are trying to control others unnecessarily. If people understood the spiritual power that is seeded within the potential of every group matrix, then they might want to begin focusing more on Unity Consciousness. The potential for working together as a council of heart-centered human beings is truly awesome. These *heart* councils would automatically become a part of the off-planet Councils of the Christ Light and everyone involved would become linked with the Spiritual Hierarchy.

Since the ego does not usually give up easily and humans generally abhor change, mankind needs a vision to move into a new relationship paradigm. It is usually difficult for the male, or the mental body, to surrender to the female, or the emotional/feeling body, in order that these new relationship possibilities be explored. Women want so much to be loved that they often give their power to men. Women need to heal the roots of their emotional fear and instability in order to be truly loved and respected by men. It is only in this healing that women can bring the fire of their spiritual compassion, power, and wisdom into the heart center, where their Higher Self abides.

Women need to be *felt* by their men, not necessarily understood. How can the mind speak to the heart? Both partners must agree to speak from the wisdom of the heart and to surrender to what is happening on a *feeling* level in order to connect on a *spiritual* level. Men and women most often communicate from a different reference base, and that has been equally frustrating to both sexes. The masculine self is inherently attracted to the mind and, therefore, to that which is less threatening and less intimate. Women are coming out of their old survival patterning enough to speak their deeper truths. They are beginning to understand that they desire intimacy with their mates above all else. Whether they are conscious of it or not, both men and women want to create a new foundation for relationships.

The core desire of many human beings who are choosing to experience more freedom and more love within their relationships is to explore intimacy through physical, mental, and spiritual union. We are just beginning to see couples who are truly co-creative and able to join together in mutual respect for each other's gifts and talents. These couples are often the ones who have made contractual soul agreements to serve as our new relationship role models.

Humanity is being given the opportunity to heal the long-standing and sorrowful battle that has existed between the sexes. This battle is not really about the problems and differences between men and women. It is about the control that the lower mind, which is based in the personal will center at the solar plexus, has had over the feeling nature of all humankind. When this schism is healed, there will be a spiritual coming together between man and woman that has not taken place throughout all of our recorded history. The desire to heal the rift between man and woman, or between the head and the heart, is one of the major facets of our current spiritual revolution. The homosexual issues that are coming forth in our world are also a great part of our redefining ourselves, our roles, our relationships, and our values.

During patriarchal cycles, both men and women are cut off from their feelings. Men express primarily from the ego at the solar plexus and women's throat chakras become dormant. The solar plexus becomes the primary power center. When war and competition become the order of the day, men cannot afford to have feelings and women go unconscious in order to avoid the pain. Men actually want love just as much as women do, but both sexes go into denial when survival and power become the main forces that are driving their motivation.

When one is living from the solar plexus, then he or she is virtually being controlled by the ego and by the reactive and survival instincts of the emotional and physical body. In sports, the solar plexus serves to fire up the body's physical power and its deep competitive urges, which were originally called into play for war and pure survival. The solar plexus does facilitate physical mastery. It can be used to amplify one's ability to function optimally, particularly under stress. However, if a man or a woman were to rely solely on this chakra for their sense of self worth, they could become identified with their physical bodies and their ego-minds as their only source of power.

A patriarchal society is focused on all that eventually brings forth death, disease, and loss of the ego's identification with the True Self. *If you are seeking ascension, then the impulse toward death and disease needs to be cleared from the body on a cellular level.* By centering one's consciousness at the heart, one definitely initiates the re-seeding of their cells with the immortality impulse of the Christ-self. The male (or solar plexus) domination within our world has muffled and repressed the deep sensitivities of the spiritual self's sole function: to create and to live from love.

When each sex is successful at re-centering in the heart, then the emotional bodies of both men and women can be free to merge without conflict. The higher feeling nature of the Christ Self can then allow the spiritual Lightbodies of the divine male and female to come together in perfect polarity. Our divine sexuality is just beginning to be understood. This understanding will come through the heart and not through the basic instincts to procreate or the desire to experience physical pleasure primarily through the genitals or the strictly tactile pleasures of the body.

As we explore the refined sensuality of our Lightbodies, we will more fully understand the polarity functions of our higher male and female selves. We will then be open to experiencing true heart love: beyond judgment, beyond competition, beyond survival, and beyond co-dependency and sexual abuse. Feelings of unconditional love have been basically dormant within all of humankind during this past patriarchal cycle. Now they are beginning to be felt for the first time in thousands of years.

Couples are already beginning to merge as one in their fifth-dimensional Lightbodies. They are unveiling some of the mysteries and challenges of higher union. The basic senses of seeing, smelling, hearing, touching, and tasting are being expanded to embrace the more subtle and refined energies that are associated with our higher bodies of Light and Love.

Real freedom and empowerment for both sexes is based on our collective challenge to surrender and merge in the Oneness. This natural order of the higher dimensions allows both sexes to meet in the Heart of the One True Self.

Higher-Self Relationship

All of the dynamics of life and unconditional love are cradled within the seed potential of each of our relationships.

Every facet of the whole of God exists within the ecstatic possibilities that relationships hold for expressing and living in the Oneness with each other and with *All That Is*. In the midst of all of this potential, many people still remain in relative isolation, often searching for greater and grander distractions for maintaining the separation. Space age technologies are certainly gifts of this age. They are tantalizing our minds into exploring new worlds, but they are also giving many people a good excuse to become even more separate. At this time in our evolution, I feel that we desperately need to balance our fast-paced lives with loving relationships or else our feeling natures will never be able to keep up with our minds!

Technologies sometimes appear to be a last ditch effort of the dark forces to keep human beings from becoming truly sovereign. Real spiritual strength comes from the heart and you can't get there through a computer. We have been at this kind of a crossroads many times before and once again our spirits are being tested to see if we can remain spiritually on target. To assure that the divine plan goes through, there are supposedly 144,000 Ascended Masters presently incarnate. However, even new age metaphysicians who must surely be a part of this band of "Masters" are still suffering from the debilitating pangs of separation. Why?

The Earth is a melting pot for beings from many different stars, planets, and other world systems. Some have come here to assist in the Earth's transition and most have come to make this great shift a part of their own evolution into higher states of consciousness. Lightworkers, who are a collective group of planetary volunteers and Starseeds, often have an innate fear of coming completely into their bodies while they are on Earth because the veils around this planet are so dense and the people here are in so much fear and denial. It has taken many years for the spiritual guardians of this planet to convince Lightworkers to embody more fully. This is not just a planetary need; it is also a personal need, since physical embodiment will allow Lightworkers to complete their own karma and their own ascension!

TO ANCHOR THE ASCENSION FREQUENCIES,

A GREAT NUMBER OF SOULS MUST AGREE

TO BE SPIRITUALLY PRESENT

WITHIN ALL ASPECTS OF THE SELF,

INCLUDING THE BODY!

It took me a long time to determine how little I was actually living here on this planet in a physical body. Though I was able to physically and mentally function on the Earth plane, I was, for the most part, spiritually absent. When I began experiencing my soul coming into my body, then I began to realize that it was going to be a tremendous process for humankind to receive the Holy Spirit into their hearts. I can see and feel when other people are not spiritually present if I am *at home* in the heart of my own God-Presence. Part of my service has been to assist people in consciously coming to Earth.

Many Lightworkers have experienced the guilt, sorrow, and fear that this planet's mass consciousness has held since its *fall* or separation from God. Many Lightworkers feel that they may have been partially responsible for the destruction of Lemuria and Atlantis.

We all exist within the influence of our collective memory fields. One thing that we all share is the fear of feeling pain. Emotional, physical, and mental anguish — actual *or* potential — keeps us at a distance from ourselves, from each other, and from the overall suffering of humankind.

While on Earth, we are each given the opportunity to magnetize others into our lives who mirror the hidden aspects of ourselves and our patterning. We attract the people and create the circumstances that we need for healing the suffering of the limited self. However, we usually do not see it this way. We continue to be faced with the same lessons over and over again, often missing opportunities to heal the pain of our past.

Many workshops have been created across the country to assist people in this clearing. It seems that most of you who are consciously working at freeing yourselves do find the individuals or groups that you need for delving into your next level of healing and expansion. Eventually, it is hoped that these often difficult and painful clearing sessions will be looked upon as a great blessing.

It is not easy for the ego-body-mind to surrender into a state of pure emotional release. It often takes a group dynamic and a facilitator for this release to occur. The support of others is also vitally important. The mind will always try to hold on to what is safe, comfortable, and familiar. If the heart remains shielded in pain, it cannot bring the spirit of your Master Self into your body.

IF YOU WANT TO AWAKEN
EVERY LIVING CELL IN YOUR BODY,
THEN YOU MUST BE WILLING
TO GO TO THE ROOT OF YOUR SUFFERING.
THIS IS THE CHALLENGE OF THESE TIMES!

It helps to remember that we are going through all of this pain in order to prepare ourselves for a dimensional shift. The only way that we are going to free ourselves and our planet is to break down the walls around our hearts. By going *through* these clearing, healing, and cleansing processes, we are literally preparing our human selves to ascend. In case you haven't noticed, people who are not spiritually oriented are also being challenged.

Most people in relationships are having difficulties because they are not in harmony with what is surfacing to be healed. Intense inner work is going on both day and night. Since we are moving out of the dominance of the left brain and its ability to make all things logical and understandable, there are times when confusion is inevitable. The emotional body is coming out of denial. You may want to cry and scream for no reason whatsoever. You are letting go of energies that have been locked in your body for years and perhaps lifetimes. You may not be able to identify where these feelings are coming from. If you are feeling pressured or confused, you may find it extremely helpful to learn how to intimately connect and communicate with your Higher Self.

Communication Tools

"If you have faith as a grain of mustard seed, you will say to this mountain, 'move' ... and nothing will be impossible to you."

— Matthew 17:20

To SUCCESSFULLY COMMUNICATE, you must first be willing to create a time for directly communing with the deepest and highest levels of your multidimensional self. If you truly want to have a spiritually intimate relationship, then you also need to know how to access and communicate with the Higher Self of your mate. You may extend the following communication techniques to include any other significant person with whom you are living or working. If you are alone, then you may wish to use this time for establishing a direct communication with your own Higher Self. You may also want to call in your spiritual guides or Master Teachers, if you feel it is appropriate for you to do so at this time.

💗 *Turn off the phone, lock all of the doors, and create a sacred space for receiving and asking questions of your Higher Self or your guides.*

If you really want to experience spiritual intimacy, you must make these sessions a priority in your life and not allow anything to interfere with your Higher Self communications.

💗 *You may choose to say a prayer for protection by asking that you be surrounded with the Diamond Light of the Cosmic Christ and the Sapphire Blue Ray of Divine Will and Protection.*

Archangel Michael and his heavenly host will amplify this protection if you call them forth to do so. You may also want to fill the room and your auric field with the Violet Ray of Transmutation. Use any prayer or affirmation which you find particularly useful for establishing and maintaining your space and the spiritual integrity of your lifestream.

💗 *Face each other and become totally aware of your breath and its ability to connect you with all aspects of your inner being, your Christ-self and your I AM Presence.*

A few minutes of conscious breathing will assist you in creating a resonant field, which will lead you into feeling the light and the love which naturally exist when you are living within the expansiveness of your Higher Self.

💗 *Close your eyes, keep breathing deeply, and consciously center all of your attention in the heart. When you feel centered and well-connected with your Heart Flame, then focus on your beloved I AM Presence as a natural extension of your heart; continue to release your stream of conscious Light until it reaches the Great Central Sun.*

Please note: If there are two or more of you doing this meditation, it may be helpful if one of you acts as a guide. Sometimes it is easier to concentrate and to go more deeply into your heart if your eyes are closed. This may be especially true if you are receiving specific information from your Higher Self or your spiritual overseers.

💗 *Extend a ray of love-filled light from your heart to the heart of your partner. Without efforting, also visualize each of your chakras being aligned, and then place your attention on a singular point of Light above your heads. Ask that this point of Light be the place at which you are each able to relate from the love, the inner knowingness, and the higher communicative faculties of the Christ-self.*

When you are doing this exercise with your mate, you may feel quite comfortable merging all of your chakras; but if you are working with a friend or a group, you may only want to align your hearts or your upper chakras. In some cases, you may only want to work together using the singular point of Light explained above.

❤ If you are doing this exercise with another and you have chosen to keep your eyes closed, then please know that *before you complete this process it is often advantageous for you to open your eyes to acknowledge how you each look and feel in this expanded state of consciousness.* Often deep love and new awarenesses come forth to be expressed during these dynamic moments of co-realization. You will know and feel the truth of your Higher Self union by your increased sense of expansiveness and love. The edges of your physical self may feel as though they have melted away.

❤ *You may desire to use this intimate time to practice communicating from specific chakras.*

For example, let us say that you want to more clearly express to your partner what is going on in your solar plexus. This third chakra is associated with issues of personal power since it is the seat of the ego-mind. The first and second chakras contain survival and sexual issues, which are equally important to clear if one is truly willing to keep the lines of communication open and flowing. The second chakra often contains the intense unspoken sorrows of the sexually abused inner child who may still be afraid to open up to its full creative capacities. You may be weak in the fifth (throat) chakra and need to develop that center in order to learn how to voice your deeper desires. You may want to improve your clarity and your ability to interpret what your heart is wanting to say. We are each learning how to spiritually hear the still, small voice of the Self within the heart.

You will always find it mutually beneficial to practice expressing what you are feeling from the truth of your heart chakra, which anchors your ability to love and to experience Cosmic Union with each other and God simultaneously. And last, but neither highest nor least, maybe you want to say something from your brow (third eye) or crown chakra, which are there to help you translate the wisdom of your Master Self. As we learn to relate to the reflections that we are feeling and seeing within each other's eyes, we are continually moving as ONE into higher and higher fields of communicative exchange.

THE DAYS AHEAD WILL REQUIRE FORTITUDE. RELATIONSHIPS WILL BE CHALLENGED AS THE HEALING PROGRESSES.

Adversity in relationships is simply pointing to the areas where the most potential exists. The desire for power and control is based on fear and internal suffering. The individualized ego-body-mind does not support *true* listening, or any kind of real communicative exchange, because that would foster Oneness and give us a taste of what naturally exists when the heart unites with the Higher Self. As you release your barriers of conflict, as you let down your shields of separation, and as you surrender into the joys of living and serving within a committed partnership, you will truly begin to witness the wonder of your co-creation and you will know the power, the love, and the wisdom that is attainable within the dynamics of Higher Self relationship.

Equality, Trust and Empowerment

When your ego surrenders into true equality with all life, then the power of trust can enter into your cells and you will experience union without fear.

THE PEOPLE IN SOME SO-CALLED PRIMITIVE CULTURES, such as the aborigines of Australia, do not have a word for *God*. They have never become aware of themselves as entities who are separate from their Creator or from each other. They have remained in harmony with the cycles of the Earth and they continue to live in natural, caring states of equality and trust. The Australian aborigines communicate interdimensionally and they have sustained their abilities to telepathically communicate with one another for thousands of years. According to Marlo Morgan's book, *Mutant Message*, which describes her experiences in Australia, the aborigines feel that we have lost our ability to speak with one another telepathically because we do not honor our inner truth and we try to protect ourselves by telling lies.

Marlo went on a *walkabout*[30] with an aboriginal tribe, whose leader told her that his people have decided to leave the planet since civilization is making it so difficult for them to remain. They are going to die out, she said, by not having any more children. When I heard this, I cried. I felt the loss of these people who have been

---

[30] An aboriginal term for barefoot journeys across the Australia outback, often lasting for months and involving no supplies or extra clothing.

demonstrating for centuries how to live, using their God-given, extrasensory faculties. My feeling is that the aboriginal people never *fell* into the third-dimensional consciousness grid. They continued to live in the fourth dimension and have, therefore, been able to sustain the attributes inherent to that plane of consciousness. The major difference between our cultures is this: their survival depends on the natural world; our survival depends on the material world!

I have listened to Marlo Morgan speak on two occasions. Although I know that there is some controversy as to whether or not her adventures are even real, I felt touched at the heart both times she spoke. I feel that she *is* a messenger who has been elected to bring some of the gifts of the aborigines to our attention before we are left to fend for ourselves. By their very simple living, these gentle tribes have taught us how to trust the Earth and the universe to provide for all of our needs. They have also let us know that we cannot work successfully with the elemental beings or the subtleties of the nature kingdom until we are willing to be still and strong enough to connect with our own inner essence.

Both planetary (geological) and human upheavals are shaking us to the very core. We are being forced to look at life and one another in a new light. If we could just succeed in moving out of scarcity thinking and competition, we could at least begin to explore what it feels like to live and love unconditionally. **There is enough — enough love, enough energy, enough money, and enough wisdom for all of us to live harmoniously! Trust, which is generally established in the first year of life, is a major factor in removing the armor of the heart's natural ability to live and love without the fear of survival (a root chakra issue).**

The influences of our forebears have imbued us for centuries with the impulse to sustain the *belief* in separation. In most of us, this has instilled an inborn (and often inexplicable) sense of fear that has become the foundation of all of our Earth-life experiences. Fear is considered a primal, root chakra issue because it taints every aspect of life until we learn how to re-parent ourselves and become sovereign beings. Many, fortunately, are doing just that.

Every life provides us with an opportunity to clear out old belief structures. One of the most powerful ways that we can release the fears that we may have around co-empowerment is to allow ourselves to honestly feel and say, "I am you." Some may balk at this idea. However, we are sharing in this Earth journey, and we are missing all that life has to offer us if we insist on maintaining a separative stance.

Equality frees new levels of co-creativity that often lay dormant beneath the competitive urges and authority issues of an unhealed solar plexus, for it is here that the ego primarily maintains its beliefs in separation. I can actually feel my solar plexus contracting when I want to stay in control. Witness your inner reactions to other people's talents and powers by watching how your mind and body honestly respond to their successes, failures, ideas, or projects. Do you find yourself expanding in love and support or do you find yourself inwardly contracting in fear by comparing your talents with theirs? If you secretly find yourself sinking into competition and into disharmony with your own sense of self worth and empowerment, then you know that you have work to do. Bless and forgive yourself for being willing to look at yourself so honestly and move on!

WHEN THE CHRIST-SELF
IS TRULY REALIZED WITHIN YOUR HEART,
YOU WILL NO LONGER NEED TO DEFEND, COMPARE,
OR COMPETE WITH ANOTHER.

If you start comparing your progress with anyone else's, you can be sure that your ego is controlling your consciousness and that you are feeling a lack of your own self worth. We are all absolutely equal and must see ourselves that way if the heart is going to be able to anchor in the True Self. If you see that you are comparing yourself with others, you can use that as an indication that your ego is still urging you to remain separated from your true God-estate.

Empowerment is consciously choosing to take responsibility for supporting the manifestation of your full-potential Self on the physical plane. The deep intention for making this commitment often comes after you have truly chosen to bring your Master Self into form. Short of that, there may be an egoic fear for survival within the third-dimensional body, which says that you are not safe enough, courageous enough, nor stable enough to be in charge of yourself.

Workshops geared to clearing the emotional body and strengthening the assertive nature can assist those who feel that they are not ready to fully manifest their power. Additionally, we often need the support of others before we feel it is safe enough to bring the immense power of our spiritual selves onto the physical plane. When you truly know that you are divine, you can afford to be absolutely human and absolutely supportive of other people's success. You will honestly feel equality in the core of your being and you will not need to speak of your successes or your failures.

Again I must say that the physical body cannot merge with the full forcefield of Love and Light that *is* the I AM Presence until most limiting patterns are released and cleared from within the emotional and mental bodies. This does not have to be as extensive a process as it may sound. You have already spent lifetimes preparing for your liberation. These are the times that are ripe for reaping the rewards of freedom. If there is resistance, there will be pain. How your ego transforms is up to you. How much drama you need to experience in order to heal your emotional body is a highly individualized matter.

It is not easy for most of us to surrender our human identities. We must be very, very courageous to give up our past beliefs and our future ideals. We must be willing to give up *everything* that we thought we were. We must lift our central focus from the ego-based solar plexus up into the soul's more authentic power base: the heart. It is only from there that we can surrender enough to realize the true Heart; it is only from there that we can begin to even glimpse what it means to live as the I AM Presence.

When the Holy Spirit enters and merges with the whole of the body, right down to the soles of the feet, then your physical, emotional, and mental bodies begin to trust they are going to be supported during your transformation. One of the first signs of this support is the total comfort that you will feel in your body. When your true Essence (the Holy Spirit of your I AM Presence) enters into your form, you will feel at home in yourself! Nothing compares with this feeling. It is what many of us have been searching for all of our lives!

Conscious Union

The fiery desire for union is reaching a climax in the hearts of all those who are driven by the soul's remembrance of the Oneness.

AFTER BELOVED MOTHER MARY AND LORD SHIVA had stripped me of all my layers of identity,[31] I felt extremely good but extremely empty. The next day I was to give a two-hour workshop at a conference retreat in Mount Shasta. I was so empty inside that I did not really feel that I could facilitate the gathering. At the final hour, however, I was filled with more than enough love and light to guide the creative visualizations and to give the workshop.

The next evening, I joined the group for a beautiful musical concert. A woman named Kathy Zavada was singing songs centered around the Divine Mother. At some point in her singing, I went into what I can only call *ecstasy*. I felt the Holy Spirit coming into my body, and I began crying and wanting to get up and hug people. Interestingly enough, however, I did not seem to want to hug just anybody.

I found myself looking for people who could really receive the love and energy that was coming through me. For the first time in my life I knew that I was really feeling the kundalini not only rising, but also descending! A great shaft of energy felt like it was going up

---

[31] This experience is described in detail in the chapter entitled "The Last Dance."

and out of the top of my head, and then it seemed to turn around and come back down through the entire trunk of my body. I was literally experiencing sexual union with my body's own polarities!

At some point I knew that if two people were actively running these ascending and descending energies simultaneously, then they would both be able to experience the kind of cosmic union that people have only dreamed of finding during sexual intercourse. We don't really need each other for raising the kundalini, but how fantastic it would be to share in these exquisite internal unions! While all of this was running through my mind and body, I also kept feeling like I was in the Himalayas and that the Masters were watching over me. They seemed to be monitoring my progress while telling me that these kinds of experiences would happen more often if I could only bring my Spirit more fully into my body.

In the hours that followed the concert, I continued to allow myself to feel totally consumed by love. This whole experience seemed to be blatantly revealing to me my very deepest desire: to feel this much love and this much of God's Life-force, or Spirit, inside of my physical body. Now the question became, "What have I really learned from this experience and how can I sustain or re-create these feelings on my own?" I seemed to be living in a state of grace and one that I might not be able to duplicate. I had definitely been shown what it feels like to embody the most powerful love that I had ever felt, and I knew that all of it was a gift from the Divine Mother!

I remain in ongoing gratitude for the living lessons that the Masters continue to give me. The ascension process now seems to involve my great desire to descend ever more fully into the body. The Masters tell me that this desire for spiritual union with the Self *within* the body is actually encoded in the Heart Flames of both men and women. This driving force for spiritual reunion has most often been relegated to the biological and often psychological need to experience sexual union. To be touched physically and to create new life is a part of the human experience. Though touch remains physically important for one's health and well being, the deep inborn desire for spiritual union is exposing an even more profound need: to internally reunite with the forces of creation.

Some Lightworkers are presently focusing their longings for a higher union onto the ancient art of Tantra. This is probably a step in the right direction, but will it really heal our deep desires for reunion with the True Self? We have exploited ourselves sexually for so many eons. We have searched for romance in all the wrong places. We have gone down the mouse maze hundreds of times, only to discover that there really is no cheese. Our rewards have been few and usually short-lived.

In my observance of hundreds of spiritual seekers, I have found that people who are trying to find God are really trying to find love. They are often looking outside to find what is truly within. We are all searching for our true Selves. When we can really just be who we are without edification, we may be able to more fully accept, see, and feel God as our Self and simultaneously as the absolute Source of all life everywhere.

Americans are a particularly lonely group of people. Loneliness is not even known in some countries. In India, for example, there is so much interaction among the people that a certain kind of intimacy exists simply by nature of the circumstances. We, however, often live in "caves" of isolation. Americans are obsessed with romantic idealism. We concentrate so much energy on how we appear physically, usually unsatisfied with what we see in the mirror. We often waste our time in superficial activities, always hoping that we will attract that perfect mate who will totally love and understand our every need.

The wounds of our remaining in the limiting thoughts of the lower self are festering with some painful outcomes. War and disease are still in our world, and emotionally we may not be any more advanced then some of our barbaric ancestors — perhaps less. All our technologies have not brought us any closer to happiness, nor have they healed the soul's deeper need to love and be loved. As a race, I feel that we are lonelier than ever.

ONE CAN MAKE NO DISTINCTION
BETWEEN GOD AND THE SELF
WHEN ONE IS ENLIGHTENED,
BECAUSE THERE IS NO LOWER MIND OR EGO
TO CREATE THE EXPERIENCE OF SEPARATION.

To be *in* God we must release all concepts that we have *about* God. All belief systems are artifacts of the separate self that soon become unnecessary and cumbersome. The challenge is to continuously remain in such a state of *now*-ness that the power of the Self does not succumb to the magnetic pull of the lower consciousness.

We do not, for the most part, know how to live from the joy of a free heart, because most of us have not yet awakened the seed of Christ Consciousness that is within the Flame of the Heart! When we do, it is a very, very momentous occasion! Emotions and even deep feelings do not necessarily come from the heart. Most often they are founded in survival, fear, pain, and need, all centered in the first three chakras. To find the true core of love, we must let go of everything that is not born of Spirit. The heart's liberation depends on our surrendering the abusive memories of the past and the unrealistic expectations of the future. Living in the purity of the present is not as easy as it sounds.

Most of us have been so poorly impressed by the relationship models of our families and our society that we decided long ago that we could only be safe if we maintained a separate stance. Many have been successful in sustaining that separateness, even within the context of their supposedly intimate relationships. Much fear of intimacy stems from not wanting to merge with another's pain or their mental or emotional discordancy. If you have not embodied your Spirit deeply enough in the self to know who you really are, then you may actually be leaving yourself open to taking on other people's disharmony.

Boundaries are important in the sense that one must always remain in integrity with the directives of the Higher Self. We can only merge perfectly when we are consciously willing to unite. This is not just a mental maneuver. I really got to see how much integrity the feeling body has during my kundalini experience at the concert in Mount Shasta. To realize that discernment exists even when one is in rapture was a very revealing revelation.

Many Eastern teachers take on the ailments of their devotees. In the Christian world, it is often thought to be loving to take on the *sorrows of the world.* In 1987, I was visited on the inner planes by four Ascended Masters. Their visit clarified for me this question of taking on the pain of others. Their energies of their God-Presence impacted me at the cellular level.

They communicated to me that I must fully release myself from identifying with the sorrows of the world. I must begin to move out of what they termed "sympathetic resonation" with the mass consciousness of the Earth. I was told that things were going to get so chaotic that to be an effective Lightworker, I must fully serve humanity by NOT identifying with its consciousness. I must, therefore, see life from an entirely new perspective. I must be "of the world and not in it,"and yet I was also shown the divinity of all life. They said that "... everyone was receiving the lessons they needed to take their next step, so do not look at the outer effects. It is all illusion ... Sustain the perfection by honoring every human being and every path."

We come here to serve as well as to experience and to master the laws of duality. Separation is NOT the truth within the higher states of being. We truly are all one! We individualize as a separate ego until we desire once again to return to the Oneness with All That Is. Since we have already chosen to become a part of this divine experiment in the individuation of God, *we must now fully incarnate as the Divine before we can return to the Absolute.* It is a great honor to be given the opportunity to master this assignment. Home is, after all, a state of unified God- Consciousness, and it can be experienced on any plane or dimension of being. Your own realization of the Self as Love will assist you in maintaining the purity of your life force.

THE CHRIST FLAME IN YOUR HEART

HAS ONE BURNING DESIRE:

TO BE IN CONSCIOUS DIVINE UNION AT ALL TIMES!

LOVE IS THE ONLY FORM OF <u>TRUE</u> COMMUNION

IN ALL THE MANY DIMENSIONS OF BEING!

The Shadow Self

"But we have this treasure in earthen vessels, that the excellency of power may be from God, and not from us. We are distressed in every way, but not overwhelmed; we are harassed on all sides, but not conquered; persecuted, but not forsaken; cast down, but not destroyed."

— II Corinthians 4:7–9
(*The Holy Bible,* Lamsa translation)

ALL RELATIONSHIPS BLESS US with the opportunity to heal our residual karma. Only while embodied can we truly be brought face to face with the people and the circumstances that we need for healing the wounds of our past. The Earth is the appropriate sphere for coming to terms with our leftover obligations, for it is here that we must forgive ourselves and others for past misuses of power, and it is here that our hearts have an opportunity to expand in compassion and wisdom.

Fortunately, we are not always dependent on finding specific past life associations or soulmates for completing our karma. We are continuously being led by our Higher Selves to find those who have matching scenarios and who can, thereby, assist us in seeing what it is we have come to learn or to heal. Although co-dependency is not what we eventually want to support, it can and often does blatantly point out to us our residual needs and patterns.

Without relationships, even unhealthy ones, we would probably never discover our weaknesses, our wounds, or our strengths. Our families and mates are especially fertile grounds for providing us with the mirrors that we need for seeing how we create our reality. They also supply us with valuable arenas for practicing loving service, which is a major facet of initiation.

When we volunteered to come to this planet, we automatically became candidates for its mastery. In the past, Earth has been looked upon as a place of exile due to its heavy veiling and its people's disassociation from their Creator. Since we are now moving out of the Kali Yuga,[32] or the darkest of ages, Earth is fast becoming the primary planet in the cosmos for providing its inhabitants with the initiatic opportunities that they need for learning how to live as the Heart of the unlimited Self.

When this mastery is undertaken in earnest, you will find that the healing of all your present and past lives begins to escalate. Old patterns that are affecting your sense of freedom and divine purpose are destined to come forward. You can always use your relationships for seeing and clearing the patterns which are no longer serving your mastery. At least some aspect of one's relationship to his or her own inner male or female is generally mirrored by one's physical plane partner. If a woman, for example, is weak in her male self, she will very often strive to find a strong male companion. She will, however, often end up with a man who perfectly reflects the weaknesses or the strengths of her own inner male.

Relationships always stimulate the unmanifested drama of the *shadow self*, which is a term used to describe that part of oneself which is usually not seen or known. The shadow self holds in denial those aspects of self that we have judged as negative or unacceptable, while we blithely project into the world a false self which we have judged as "acceptable." Often we expect our mates or — even worse — our children to play out the roles of our shadow selves.

I have witnessed the children of parents who are extremely oriented to the spiritual side of life. These parents literally wore all white clothing almost every day. The children were playing out the shadow selves of their parents by drinking alcohol, taking drugs,

---

[32] A Yuga is a cycle of time that spans roughly 26,000 years. The word *Kali* refers to an especially dark or difficult cycle of evolution.

and having sex at an early age. The parents truly had no interest in alcohol, drugs, or sex, but somehow their children felt that they had to express the feelings that their parents were not willing to acknowledge in themselves. These feelings could include anger, sorrow, rage, or any number of repressed emotions.

It is up to each of us to stop projecting the unacknowledged "negative" parts of ourselves onto others. It really takes some deep willingness to even see the play of the shadow self. If we could put more energy into seeing and healing the whole self, and thereby start living as the radiant loving beings that we truly are, then the children of this world would have a much greater chance of realizing their freedom. To make a true shift in the mass mind in the next few years, children need to be able to get on with their own soul contracts. As parents, we can no longer expect our children to fulfill our dreams. They must have the *emotional space* to become clear enough to fulfill their own life's mission.

The realizations that are implied by the presence of a dark or hidden self are often difficult to endorse unless you understand that there is *"gold in them thar hills."* And that gold, even if it is black gold, contains tremendous creative energy. The shadow self is related to the whole of the collective unconscious and it is, therefore, one of the major keys that we have for unlocking our full potential energy.

THE SUCCESS OF OUR HEART INITIATION
IS ACTUALLY DEPENDENT UPON
OUR RELEASING THE POWER THAT IS CONTAINED
WITHIN THE RESOURCES OF THE SHADOW SELF.

The shadow self is the treasure house that we need for fully incarnating as conscious beings. We cannot transform our physical beings without its wisdom and its strength. Our collective memory banks, a part of the unconscious realms of the shadow self, are filled with thoughtforms about romance and love. This planet thrives on romantic idealism. Illusions have become the food of our materialistic world, while we remain starved for honest communication and deeper intimacy. We have come to an ideal crisis point for reprioritizing our values.

To merge with a physical plane mate is a highly intimate and intricate blending of life forces and liquid light essences. Our subtle bodies are sending waves of light and energy into our partner's body. These energies contain the programming of our unconscious worlds. They are often filled with pictures of abuse, abandonment, grief, and loss. These thoughtforms contain all of the unexpressed feelings and unmet desires that we have brought with us from our past. Within the context of sexual intercourse, we are choosing to open ourselves up to the realms of each other's unconscious. This is one way of getting to know each other's shadow self.

It is important, however, that one understand what it is he or she is undertaking in becoming physically intimate. Even sleeping next to someone involves a blending of energies, for it is during the night that most interdimensional work and education is taking place. It is vitally important that one clear the day's energies before entering sleep, and that each bed partner be free of any and all negativity towards each other and the world. It may be necessary to create a light shield between yourself and your mate so that you do not get so involved in each other's inner worlds and dreams. By doing this, you can more easily eliminate confusion and be more responsible for decoding the messages of your own dreams.

Mastery involves our being able to consciously manifest and maintain our own realities. We must move above and beyond receiving and accepting other people's projections as our truth. One of my greatest challenges has been how to maintain intimacy without identification with other people. Empathy has been defined as "the capacity for experiencing as one's own the feelings of another." I am finally learning how to become compassionately involved with others and passionately involved with my mate without truly identifying with their thoughts or feelings.

I have always been able to see others in the highest spiritual sense, knowing that all else is temporal and based on illusion. I am now learning to see how the human expressions of one's own self must also be understood and embraced in order to live here with more compassion and understanding. It seems paradoxical that one can be on this Earth plane, experience true intimacy, and yet not have to identify with or take on anyone or anything that is rooted in limitation or separation.

The exercises for communication given earlier in this section are the most useful that my husband and I have found for staying clear with one another on all issues of mutual importance. For emotional clearing, we have found that honesty is still the best policy. To come together physically, we must both be in absolute integrity with ourselves and each other. This is not very difficult if we are really living in our truth. When our relationship is clear, then love flows naturally and physical union simply becomes the desire to include our bodies with our feelings of mutual love, increasing joy, and ongoing respect. It seems to be a natural calling to come together sexually and to touch each other's bodies while we are still within the blessedness of these physical forms.

We have also discovered that as we relate more and more consciously with our Higher Selves, we are simultaneously experiencing an augmentation in our desires for more intimacy. We are wanting to create more time for focused communication and more time for conscious touching. These sessions often do *not* include coming together sexually. As we explore the more subtle levels of intimacy, we are also beginning to experience higher and higher forms of interdimensional union. It has been probably thousands of years since we exercised our abilities to consciously merge our light essences in this fashion.

After we make a conscious alignment between our Higher Selves, we often become bathed in violet, magenta, pink, gold, opalescent, and sometimes diamond light. This light *bathing* generally occurs while we are sitting upright facing one another. The colors flood us with celestial sounds, sometimes heard and always sensed. These colors are inwardly visible to both of us as they stream between our bodies, filling us with love, ecstasy, and the wisdom of our Higher Selves. Back and forth they stream ... sometimes we can only feel the blessings of their healing energies, but we always know that our intense longings to be spiritually nourished are being fulfilled.

This *light streaming* can go on as long as we wish and it often, but not always, occurs during our Higher Self communication sessions. Light streaming frequently takes place when we are lying next to each other in bed. Our feeling bodies are influenced and directed by our most prominent thoughts and desires. That is how the mind and the heart work together. We are naturally absorbed and attracted by the dimensional frequencies to which our consciousness has been attuned. The thoughts and feelings that are stored within an *unexpressed and unacknowledged* shadow self can consume a great deal of our energy. We are, once again, multi-dimensional expressions of the One Self and we are always choosing what, where, and how we want to live and how we want to create our realities.

If we transition from this plane filled with incomplete desires, then these desires will act as seeds which will remain planted in the soil of the Earth, awaiting your return and your nourishment. This will continue until you no longer leave the remains of your longings in the third-dimensional level of creation. If Earth does indeed make her transition into a new dimensional frequency, then those who are bound to their third-dimensional bodies and desires will most probably reincarnate onto other planets which will support their needs.

This means that by our thoughts, feelings, and actions, we are now making choices as to how and where we want to live after we leave this planet. Whether you return to Earth or not, you may want to choose to be free from the confines of duality which continue to play such a major role on the third and fourth dimensions. The forces of duality have such a magnetic pull on the consciousness of most humans that it takes an intense desire to free oneself from the drama of this world.

We are being challenged to embrace the dark side of the self as a part of what has been supporting and creating life on the third dimension *as we have known it.* Being willing to *witness* the Self on every level of its expression is a great step towards becoming liberated from the binding judgments of the limited mind. However, being willing to *embrace* the unlovable aspects of the self is an even greater step towards self-mastery. To move into the fifth dimension, a Heart Initiate must master the inherent energies that are within the dynamics of polarity on both the third and fourth dimensions. *Never forget: there is a light behind every shadow!*

A New Relationship Paradigm

" ... and because of the growth of iniquity, the love of many will become cold."

—St. Matthew 24:12
(*Holy Bible*, Lamsa translation)

IT IS AT ONCE A WONDERFUL AND MYSTERIOUS ADVENTURE to be so aligned with my partner one day and then the next day to find our relationship completely out of harmony. Usually it is necessary for both my husband and me to take space at that point, knowing that when these difficult times present themselves we simply need to realign with the Self in order to come back together with more inner attunement. One or both of us is usually getting pushed into separation and conflict because we did not communicate or take care of our imbalances soon enough.

We must forgive ourselves for occasionally creating thoughts, feelings, and actions which promote separation. It is, however, **not** the truth of the Self. We are moving into a time and place where these inner battles between the mind and the heart (which are being reflected within our outer relationships) will be no more. We are now in a cycle where we are being asked by our spiritual overseers and our own Higher Selves to create a new paradigm for our relationships. Fortunately, there are some dedicated souls in this world who are acting on their desire to create this paradigm.

WE HAVE BOWED TO THE KNOWLEDGE OF THE MIND.

NOW WE MUST BOW WITH EQUAL PASSION

AND DELIBERATION

TO THE WISDOM OF THE HEART.

For this evolutionary shift to be successful, the intellectual aspect of the mind must become a *willing* servant to the wisdom of the heart. Until the mind and the heart become supportive companions, there will be no rest nor freedom from bondage. This is a difficult undertaking for both men and women, especially those who are mentally-oriented. However, the true ecstasy of co-creative union cannot exist until the ego-mind is dissolved into the True Self. Even religious idealism must be released. All fears and root survival issues must be surrendered into the heart, and it takes some real dedication and deep faith to accomplish this.

As the old age makes way for the new millennium, we are in the process of redefining how we can create more meaningful relationships and how we can fulfill our deepest desires for expressing that which is real and true between us. Our memories of living within the realms of illumined truth are being stimulated to release all of the separative patterning which has kept us from realizing how we can truly live together in harmony and joy.

THE FEAR OF SURRENDERING INTO

EVER DEEPER LEVELS OF INTIMACY

HAS HISTORICALLY BEEN FAR GREATER

THAN OUR DESIRES FOR BECOMING EVEN CLOSER.

The fears that we have recorded within our individual and collective unconscious have deprived us of really trusting one another or the flow of life itself. Because such a great portion of humankind does not live from the Heart, we have had good reason to lose our trust in the words and actions of others. Until there is a great shift in the mass consciousness, it may be very challenging to really establish trust in your dealings in the material world. Remember that your projections create your reality. If you expect others to treat you fairly, you will be blessed with having them do so. To shift our collective consciousness, we must start with our individual projections!

To create a new paradigm, we also need to utilize the *power* aspect of love. An assertive action may be very important for breaking up an existing pattern. Remember how Jesus used his fervor to shock the money changers out of their destructive and mindless behavior. His "tough love" was used to demonstrate how those involved were so attached to materialism that they had lost sight of the higher values of life. In the Eastern religion of Hinduism, God is defined as having three distinct aspects: the Creator, the Preserver, and the Destroyer. This lesson that Jesus gave to us vividly demonstrates how one must occasionally use the *destructive* aspect of God's love to dissolve and change a loveless activity. This allows room for God's creative force to re-enter the hearts of all those involved. To bring the power of your Christ-self into active manifestation by speaking and acting on what you know to be the truth is a great part of creating the new relationship paradigm.

We would hope that fear does not have to bleed over into our primary relationships. For many people, however, the idea of surrendering to another human being, even in the name of love, only brings up past pictures of loss, paralyzing fear, grief, and pain. A lover provides us with a means for releasing the confines of the mind long enough to experience the pleasures of the feeling world. Most people *only* allow themselves to experience complete vulnerability during lovemaking. The rest of the time they remain controlled by the fear-based projections of the ego-body-mind.

Surrendering into our feelings (or the vulnerable inner-child self) appears to be risky, and indeed it truly is if we continue to define our actions based solely on the history of our collective emotional, mental, and physical abuse. Our spiritual overseers are pleading with us to create new perspectives that will allow us to explore alternative ways of being together and perhaps even of staying together! The excitement and enthusiasm that eventually *appears* to deteriorate between even the best of lovers generally has nothing to do with how well one mate is pleasing another.

THE COMMON DISSATISFACTIONS FOUND WITHIN
SO MANY RELATIONSHIPS ARE NOT EXTERNAL:
THEY ARE INTERNAL, FEAR-BASED
RESPONSES TO THE PAST.

The new paradigm is completely dependent on our seeing our relationships from an entirely new perspective. The past fears and the future expectations that we project onto ourselves and each other blind us to our immediate potentials for divine exchange and true intimacy. There is a great tendency to avoid intimacy in our present-day culture because most people have an incredible accumulation of fear-filled memories based on years and lifetimes of *bad* relationship experiences. The answer appears to lie in the great courage that it is going to take to be unrelenting in our willingness to go through the fire of purification.

In relationships we are always given the opportunity to let go of our defenses and our masks and to walk the fires of intimacy. To purge the self of all of its egoic illusions, we must swim against the current, for nothing in this world supports our living from and as the Heart of our True Self. We must have the courage to see ourselves impersonally. To master this level of objectivity, we must be willing to live in truth. The primal roots of our pain will naturally surface if we are willing to let go of our ideas about our self-image. This will also involve our being unattached to the mental concepts, the belief systems, and the opinions of others.

It is impractical to suppose that human beings will stop having concepts, beliefs, and opinions about themselves and others, but it is imperative at this time that we balance our mental constructs with our deeper emotional needs and desires if we are going to create a new paradigm for our relationships. The mental programming of both men and women often becomes the battleground that keeps partners from experiencing warmth and support in times of need. This tendency snuffs out intimacy and creates increasing separation within the self, as well as within the relationship.

Our minds can be used to create an environment for intimacy, but we must clearly define our primary intentions if we are not to become sidetracked in intellectualism. When the challenges of intimacy are being consciously met by both individuals, then problems can be looked upon as very integral parts of their transformation into the Heart of the One Self.

THE INTENTION TO CREATE AND MAINTAIN INTIMACY
MUST BE A PASSIONATE ONE
IF WE ARE GOING TO SUCCEED IN CREATING
A NEW RELATIONSHIP PARADIGM
FOR OURSELVES AND THOSE WHO FOLLOW.

Is it realistic to assume that we, as evolving humans, will actually be able to maintain intimacy in such a chaotic world? Within the realms of the third-dimensional mind, it does not even appear to be a remote possibility. Within the higher mind of the Master Self, however, it is an ever-abiding *fact*. We are forever in the midst of subtle energy exchanges with everyone and everything. We are even intimately connecting with all those people, places, and reflective experiences that come into our minds!

As we become more aligned with our Higher Selves, we will not be so easily shaken out of our heart centers by an inharmonious environment or by the imbalanced consciousness of another. That is when we truly become anchors for the Spiritual Hierarchy; that is when we really start shifting the mass consciousness out of its limited, dualistic thinking; that is when joy overcomes all the hidden roots of fear, and that is when we experience dipping even deeper into the waters of true intimacy!

LIVE AS THE LIGHT AND THE LOVE
THAT FOREVER FULFILLS YOUR DESIRE
TO BE EMBRACED WITHIN THE JOY,
THE ECSTASY, AND THE INTIMACY OF THE BELOVED.

Part Four

LIGHTBODY

ALIGNMENT

An Interdimensional Experience

*"Seek ye first the kingdom of God and His righteousness,
and all these things shall be added unto you."*

— Matthew 6:33

IN ORDER TO ENGAGE in interdimensional exchanges with Ascended Masters or Cosmic Beings, one is sometimes transported into what is called a *Merkabah*.[33] These vehicles of Divine Light have nothing whatsoever to do with extraterrestrial beings or their spaceships. Merkabahs are geometric fields of Divine Light created by Ascended Masters and high level Cosmic Beings in order for them to spiritually align the physical, emotional, mental, and etheric bodies of third- and fourth-dimensional humans with their higher Christ-conscious bodies of Light. Merkabahs are *forcefields* that sustain the perfection of God's Love and Light. They are sometimes set above power vortices as permanent stations for maintaining the Christ Light, and they are sometimes used as mobile vehicles for creating personal and planetary vibrational adjustments.

Merkabahs are *living* templates, or temples of Light. When we are within their forcefield, our subtle bodies are quickened. The immortal frequencies that are carried in our Light structures are being stimulated to remind us of our parts in the Divine Plan. We are being blessed with the presence of Merkabahs because we are shifting our bodies into a new dimension.

---

[33] In J. J. Hurtak's *Keys of Enoch*, Merkabah is defined as a Divine Light Vehicle used by the Masters to probe and reach the faithful in the many dimensions of the Divine Mind.

Cosmic Beings do not work with people who are only curious. Ascended Masters generally contact Lightworkers to remind them that they have a pre-birth soul agreement to manifest some aspect of the Divine Plan. Before we are invited to enter these *Ships of Light,* we are observed to see whether we can maintain a certain degree of balance within our emotional, mental, and physical bodies. Occasionally, one of the larger Merkabahs will come into the Earth's atmosphere to work with spiritual initiates.

It has generally been difficult for me to speak or to write about my personal experiences. I am now being guided, however, to share with you my first and most powerful exchange with Cosmic Beings inside of a Merkabah forcefield. In the 1970s, I was taken aboard a jewel-like vehicle of pure light substance, which I now know was a Merkabah. I believe that I was primarily brought aboard to align my fifth-dimensional Lightbody with my I AM Presence. The purpose of this experience seemed to be to bring my Christ-self and my Presence into more harmony with the chakras in my subtle energy body.

This all began while I was living in Marin County, California. A friend and I decided to take a walk and to meditate on top of Mount Tamalpais, near Mill Valley. After a few hours, I decided to lie down in a meadow near the top of the mountain. Shortly after I lay down, I felt the presence of several Light Beings who seemed to be standing around me in a circle. They telepathically asked me if I wanted to come with them. I had never experienced anything like this but, since I felt nothing but absolute love and harmony, I answered in the affirmative. They projected a powerful field of light which seemed to be helping me to separate out from my physical body. For a moment I was a little frightened, as I felt an intense pressure upon my body and a sense of becoming increasingly more dense and heavy. Suddenly there was a sound, like a rubber band snapping, and I knew that I was no longer in my body or on the Earth.

I felt light and free. I knew that I was being transported into another dimension. I was told telepathically that I had been taken out beyond the Van Allen radiation belt, which seems to mark the edge of the Earth's gravitational fields. In looking back, I now feel that it was probably important for me to be taken out of the lower astral aura of the planet. Suddenly we stopped moving through space, and I became conscious of myself in a subtle Lightbody. I was lying face up on a table beneath a huge crystal which appeared to be suspended in mid-air. It covered my body from my head to the top of my legs.

The major point of the crystal's central facet seemed to be especially aligned with the heart and sternum area of my subtle body. The crystal may have been solid or it may have been made up from a holographically-projected light substance. I do not really know, since I did not reach up and touch it. After lying under the crystal for a few minutes, I was asked to rise.

As I stood up, my interdimensional vision embraced the most beautiful, loving, radiant beings I could ever have imagined. As I looked into their brilliant opalescent-like forms, I gradually became overwhelmed by their absolute love and I slumped to the floor in tears of ecstatic joy. It was truly the closest I had ever come to seeing God.

The *crystal alignment* seemed to be assisting me in sustaining my interdimensional sight. However, my guides informed me that if I fell into too much emotional excitement, I would lose visual contact. I was then asked to rise up and to stand facing them while they aligned and energized my chakras. I was constantly feeling their unbelievable love as they proceeded to project prismatic rays of diamond-like light into each one of my chakras in a very precise manner, starting at the base of my spine. I see now that they were actually attuning me to the higher frequencies of my *own* Lightbody. How amazing it all was!

I was shown by these radiant beings how to receive healing and information through rays of *diamond light,* which projected out from the center of their foreheads in very distinctive prismatic beams. These rays of light seemed to come from their eyes as well. Their two eyes seemed to be connected with an unseen third eye in their forehead, creating an energy field which appeared to be crystalline and prismatic. Although I was constantly being healed just by inter-acting with these Beings, I was especially receiving their great healing gifts wherever their prismatic beams were being focused into my body.

At the time, I thought that I was being given a visual demon-stration of how communication occurs telepathically on the higher dimensions and how Light Beings heal others who are out of align-ment with their Higher Self. Now, after all of these years, I am beginning to understand that these beings were actually showing me how to more consciously heal and telepathically communicate on the third dimension as well!

I have since been told that this is how the Essenes healed in Jesus' time, and that we can all employ the powerful use of our All-Seeing or third eye in such a fashion. I am told further that we can promote this healing in another by visualizing and projecting *perfection* into the desired area. Since the astral or etheric body is most closely aligned with our subtle anatomy and our chakras, this is often where the work needs to be accomplished. The higher Lightbodies are already in Divine Order.

While on board the Merkabah, there were deep connections made on many levels of exchange. I was certainly not aware of any-thing being put *into* my astral body. However, it is highly possible that I had some geometric encodings activated or released which were already within my subtle body. These encodings contain geometric language keys which are set to be released at certain times in order to assist us in making our dimensional shift.

I want to emphatically share with you that the level of love trans-mission coming from these Cosmic Beings was beyond anything I had ever experienced. Every particle of their Lightbodies emanated only the purest love. Their forms were filled with an opalescent Light substance which was permeated with only the slightest amount of pastel color. All within them swirled about in living Light. They had no organs, hair, or specific clothing, but they did seem to have on some sort of seamless garment made of iridescent Light substance.

Now I have come to understand that these Beings were actually showing me that the higher feeling body of the I AM Presence is actually opalescent, or opal in frequency. When the astral or etheric body is cleared, it can then reflect the perfect Light of the *I AM Presence*. This was all a part of the instruction that they were presenting to me while I was aboard the Merkabah. A whole block of information was given to me during this experience. It unfolds as necessary.

Several weeks later, these same radiant Beings appeared and asked me to look into a mirror. In that glorious moment, I was able to see that I also had the same kind of interdimensional body. I believe that my spiritual guardians were allowing me to see the radiant form of my own I AM Presence in its interdimensional capacity. We are truly functioning in many different realities and dimensions simultaneously!

# The Language of Light and Sound

"From our perspective, the most significant intention for the process of meditation is to facilitate the opening of a pathway, or channel, between dimensions. Once a passageway has been established, through the process of meditation, then communication can easily be transmitted and received between dimensions." [34]

ON THE FIFTH AND SIXTH DIMENSIONS, communications are projected through glorious prismatic rays of opalescent and diamond light, which directly pass or arc information into all those who are willing or capable of receiving these vibrational light waves. This divine Love and Light substance can also be passed to and fro on the third dimension. We are really just learning how we can communicate using all of the sacred rays, and how we can be sustained and nourished by light and sound.

Pure crystalline light seems to be used to transfer information in all interdimensional exchanges. It is much clearer than the spoken word because it eliminates the misunderstandings that so often occur during verbalization. Words themselves are founded in duality. As we express more and more from the wisdom of the Heart, we are finding new ways to communicate. All that is hidden might as well come to the surface because what we are *really* saying is increasingly being *seen* and *heard* by the inner *eye* and *ear* of many of our listeners.

---

[34] *Abraham Speaks Vol. V: A New Beginning, Handbook for Joyous Survival,* by Jerry and Esther Hicks.

Whenever we receive interdimensional communication, we are naturally translating the *Language of Light and Sound*. I receive large blocks of information in a few moments. This material has to be translated if it is to be written or communicated in our language. The more the lower bodies are balanced within the threefold Flame of the heart, the easier it is to receive information through the Higher Self from the I AM Presence or the Ascended Masters.

There is Light and Sound encoding within our cells and within the blueprints of our etheric body. We contain mysteries, much like the Sphinx carries hidden keys, and they are *all* going to be *uncovered* at some sacred and appropriate moment in time. We are specifically monitored by the Spiritual Hierarchy to determine when these encodings can be released.

Many Lightworkers have been sent to the power points of the Earth to heal and cleanse the dense astral aura that so often encases these areas in the darkness of the past. These journeys are not usually comfortable or easy on the participants. Often the people who are sent to clear specific power vortices are those who have had past associations with the area involved. The aura around ancient civilizations is often filled with the grief of human sacrifice and other misuses of power that were displayed by the priests and leaders of the time.

Now we know that real authentic power comes from the heart and its alignment and attunement with all of the sacred *power points* which exist quite naturally within, upon, and above the Earth. The chakras of this planet are in line with the stellar forcefields, or grid maps, which contain the energy vortices that connect our planet and our bodies to the greater cosmos. We are intimately connected with our Earth's ascension. We are all aligning our inner and outer selves with our collective *Cosmic Light* encoding. All of our personal and planetary power points are waiting to be activated so that we can be more consciously united with our universe.

There are stone structures upon the Earth, particularly those at ancient sacred sites, which are acting as storehouses of information.

You also have information which is carefully stored within the bones of your body. I received this information after visiting Avebury in England. During a group meditation, I suddenly found myself exclaiming, *"Our bones contain the most condensed amounts of information that we have in our bodies, and they are directly related to the storehouses of information that are encoded within the sacred stones on the planet."*

I have since learned that it is *sound* which will be most instrumental in releasing this encoded information. "When you allow sound to move through you, it unlocks a doorway and allows information to flood into your body. It also penetrates the ground, affecting the vibrations of Earth and allowing a rearrangement of a molecular alignment of information to take place. Those of you who use sound when you are doing healing work bring about a rearrangement of the molecular structure and create an opening for information to flood in. This kind of work will become more and more profound."[35]

Most of the inhabitants of this planet have lost connection with their intergalactic heritage. Some Native American tribes, such as the Hopi, the Navajo, and the Cherokee are all well aware of their celestial ancestors. We, however, have mostly forgotten how to communicate with the Cosmic Brotherhoods of Light who are always overseeing our personal and planetary evolvement. These interdimensional beings are now working with us to stimulate our cosmic memory banks. These Cosmic Beings are aligning us with the creative energies of the Great Central Sun so that we can remember entire files of information. We are learning how to decode the languages of light and sound.

Much of this work is done while we are sleeping or relatively unconscious. However, we can and will retrieve blocks of this information when we are deemed emotionally stable enough to anchor the high energy frequencies that are associated with these cosmic encodings. Sounds are also being sent to all Lightworkers, and these

---

[35] *Bringers Of The Dawn: Teachings from the Pleiadians,* by Barbara Marciniak

are *tuning* our four lower bodies so that they can become more sensitive and equipped to handle the harmonics of the higher dimensions. You may have been hearing lots of ringing or high-pitched noises in your ears. These are cosmic sound waves that are acting as tuning forks for aligning our physical bodies with our Lightbodies. These sounds are releasing the contractions in our bodies; when you hear them, just be still and let them do their transformational work.

It is necessary for us to accelerate the energies within our etheric bodies before we can raise our denser vehicles into the higher frequencies. Many Light Beings are assisting us in the etheric realms as they are also being directly affected by our transition.

OUR ASCENSION INVOLVES
MANY OTHER DIMENSIONS OF LIFE
WITHIN THIS UNIVERSAL SYSTEM.

My greatest physical experience of a large Merkabah vehicle occurred when I was visiting Tiberius, Israel, in April of 1986. It took the beloved Mother Mary and her angels and Archangel Michael and his heavenly hosts three days to prepare me to interface with the Cosmic Christ on the Sea of Galilee. My nervous system was literally rewired by the angels of Light. My emotional body went through heaven and hell before the Merkabah finally arrived. I truthfully had no idea that I was preparing to meet the Christ.

It was in the wee small hours of the morning that I abruptly found myself *seeing* into another dimension. I was suddenly looking at the night sky right through the roof of the hotel where my husband and I were staying. As I stared in disbelief, three Light vehicles zoomed overhead and I shouted to my husband, "They're here! They're here!" My body nearly levitated right through the ceiling when I saw and felt the tremendous impact of these three triangular ships of Light.

I was extremely exhausted from all the previous day's preparations and lack of sleep. I had been shown many layers of the Akasha since the beginning of time. I had been invited the day before to work with Archangel Michael in clearing some karma inside of the Earth. We traveled through volcanic tubes to cleanse astral accumulations from the planet's internal auric fields. This is no easy task, and it all took its toll on my physical and subtle bodies. However, I knew that this was the moment that I had been unconsciously preparing for, and now I needed to be alert.

I asked my spiritual overseers what they wanted me to do. I was informed that I should wrap up in a blanket and go outside and focus on the Sea of Galilee. As I stood on the deck of our hotel overlooking the vast night sky, I felt an immense pulsing in the air. My spiritual vision was again reactivated and I saw the huge Merkabah vehicle, literally breathing with Living Light as it hovered over the entire Sea of Galilee. There were large beams of Light crossing each other as they lit up the surface of the water. They seemed to be stabilizing the ship and anchoring it into the sea. The sky seemed to come alive, and the whole area was transformed into holograms of Living Light. That was the beginning of several hours of communication, using only Light and holographic flame-like images.

The Cosmic Christ emerged from the Merkabah in a radiant, golden-white, Cosmic Lightbody. He spoke to me telepathically by directing his Light-encoded information into my cells. He did this while *standing* and *walking* on the surface of the Sea of Galilee. He confirmed for me his identity as the Christ by moving his Lightbody over to Capernum and then to the Mount of Beatitudes. When his Cosmic Body merged with where I knew he had been physically in his life as Jesus, there was an explosion of light, creating a bright, star-like pattern which lasted for several seconds.

The Christ communicated with me using a direct heart-to-heart energy link. I now believe that the angels who had rewired me the day before were actually preparing my body and my nervous system so that I would not burn out during these communications. Sometimes I would get so amplified by the energies of the Christ *and* the Merkabah that I would start to feel as though I was going to faint or pass out. Sometimes I would plead with Jesus/Sananda to please let me rest for a few moments. I simultaneously prayed that if I closed my eyes he would still be there when I opened them again. My heart would leap in joy when I found that he was still there after my little naps.

He gave me stories and information about the past and the future. He told me how important it was at this time in our history to come together in groups. He portrayed the people of Earth as small white lights gathering in circles on top of the Mount of Beatitudes. The Lightbody of the Christ was a brilliant golden-white. Over and over again, he would bring his body up from the Sea of Galilee and place it within the circles of the Children of Light on top of the mountain. He seemed to be wanting to communicate to me that he would bring his Love and Light into these groups, and that his consciousness could thereby be felt and experienced by all those present. In this way, he implied, he could enter the hearts of all those willing to come together in the name and vibration of the Christ.

As the sun began to rise in the early morning sky, I knew that my time for being with the Christ in this way was drawing to a end. I asked him to please come closer and to embrace me. He told me that if he came too near, I would ascend on the spot because my physical body would not be able to withstand being in such close proximity to his Cosmic Lightbody. I, of course, would have liked the ascension alternative. However, he did send a literal wave of radiant pink energy out from his Lightbody, which enfolded me in the pure essence of his Love. I wept uncontrollably in realizing that I might never see him like this again. My body was wrenched by the letting go. In a parting plea, I asked him from the sincere naiveté of my heart if I could go with him, if I could go home to God right now. He answered me by saying, "No, you must do it this time ... you must do as I have done before you. We are always together in the One that we are." This encounter changed me forever. He left me with the invocation which I have given to you in the second-to-last chapter of this book.

The geometric keys for communicating with the Language of Light may not be the same for everyone. Most Lightworkers are expediting this decoding process by opening their hearts, thereby establishing a more direct and conscious communication with the wisdom of the Christ-self. These Light-encoded translations are also being made within the seed crystal in the *Secret Place of The Most High*, which is in the center of the skull.

As the lower bodies are being cleared, Lightworkers are becoming more adept at receiving information directly from their I AM Presence. Keep in mind, however, that all of this is only accomplished through the GRACE OF GOD! Much of the Language of Light and Sound is coming through the new Diamond Light which was released in 1988. *Diamond* is the closest color that can be given to describe this new Ray. It comes to us in very intense and generally invisible particles of Light, which are smaller than dust particles but larger than neutrinos.

The thirteenth, or *Diamond Ray*, can be used for creating a geometric forcefield around an individual or a group. I have been guided to call this forcefield a *Diamond Ascension Merkabah*.[36] It consists of twelve facets pointing upward and twelve facets pointing downward. It protects the purity and integrity of the Cosmic Christ energies for all those involved. This particular matrix assists one in sustaining the Christ vibration while keeping the spine aligned with the true axis of the Earth. If I am traveling interdimensionally, either

---

[36] Detailed information on how to create and use this merkabah is now available on audio tape. *Ascension Merkabah*, by Julianne Everett, can be ordered directly through Oughten House Publications or through your local metaphysical bookstores.

alone or with a group, I always use the Diamond Merkabah, since I have found it to be tremendously powerful and it gives everyone a centralized field for focusing their energies. The Ascended Masters have asked me to place a sphere of all thirteen rays of the Cosmic Christ Light around the Merkabah to assure that it resonates with the purity of the Great Central Sun, wherein the Languages of Light and Sound originate.

 Journey into Oneness

"Trust in the Lord with all your heart, and lean not on your own understanding; in all your ways acknowledge Him, and He shall direct your paths."

— Proverbs 3:5,6

ONLY WE, AS EMBODIED AND CONSCIOUS LIGHTWORKERS, can make the call for our individual and collective freedom. Although I have received much assistance from interdimensional beings, I do not believe that we are actually going to be saved or carried off by beings from other planets or dimensions. The Ascended Masters and other Cosmic Beings working with the Christ are assisting us in understanding how we can move forward into a new alignment with our Source. These beloved Beings are volunteering their services to awaken us and to elicit our involvement on a more conscious level.

God gave us the Grace to become fully manifested Beings of Love and Light. We were given this wondrous planet to enjoy our physicality and to learn the creative laws that support a material existence. We have been spiritually conceived as a microcosmic universe, and so we are also here to learn something about the Cosmic Laws that support the greater universe. These Laws that sustain harmony and balance within the heavens maintain our Lightbodies, allowing us to create in the higher dimensions. Our physical and subtle bodies are nourished by the substance of the starry dimensions as well as by the substance of the Earth.

When we received the gift of individuality and of free will, we also received the gift of serving this planet as conscious Cosmic Beings in harmony with *all of* the Laws of Creation. We have the power and the responsibility for redeeming any of our creations that do not support the Law of The One, also known as the Law of Love. The *duality war* only seems to be taking place on the third and fourth dimensions, so that is where this redemptive work needs to take place.

I'm told by my Ascended Master Teachers that the decision to experiment with duality and conscious volition was made by all those who chose to come to planet Earth, and that human beings are going to become much more conscious co-creators from having been here. We have learned what it feels like to live from the ego-based ideas and feelings of the lower self. We have felt the lonely desperation that comes from being totally separated from our hearts, from each other, and from God. Now we have the opportunity to ascend — to lift our focus up into the heart, to live here on Earth as the Higher Self, and to manifest from Divine Feeling and Divine Wisdom while totally embracing our uniquely human expression of the One True Self.

The heart is the door to our first level of freedom. It is where we begin to translate our physical bodies into Light. It is where we learn how to heal the duality that has taken us into such density. The lower chakras are very useful and we need their energies to be fully empowered and spiritually embodied, but they were not intended to dominate our lives. We have been stretched like rubber bands out to the furthest reaches of separation. Now that rubber band is being released, and we are being *snapped back* much more quickly than it took to get us so far away from Source.

We are, paradoxically, in this initiation process alone and together. Most of us do need a certain amount of love, recognition, and support while living in a material world. The more we know who and what we are about, the less we need confirmation from others. It is always nice to be appreciated for who we are and for what we have come to give to life. When we leave this planet, however, we probably leave alone, as free emissaries of Light and Love. Time will tell if we can ascend with others or not.

When the heart is activated, it allows us to live in a world where the ego no longer has to define, support, and defend its separative position. Some people will begin their journey into Oneness by reading and going to teachers to increase their spiritual understanding. Some will want to heal their emotional suffering and they will be motivated to enter into various forms of therapy. Some will consciously decide not to go into the pain at all. Some people honestly do not appear to be suffering as individuals or as nuclear families. We cannot help but see, however, the mass suffering that humanity is now outpicturing for us in so many sectors of the world.

We have a deep collective longing to ascend into the freedom of the Heart. Each of us can decide if we want to be a part of this personal and planetary healing process. Real transformation is movement into the unknown. *Oneness* is such a frightening prospect for the ego. It is like telling someone that they are going to be dissolved into a sea of nothingness, where there is no individuality and no possibility for creative expression. We desired incarnation in order to love and to be loved, in order to serve and to express the absolute *uniqueness* of our individualized gifts.

It is NOT freedom to have to live around any co-dependency issues. It is NOT freedom to live in the sorrow, anger, and fear of the wounded inner child, and it is NOT freedom to be in any state of imbalance between the inner male and female. When the dependency on others is healed and the inner wounded child is found, re-parented, and eventually loved free, then we have a chance of healing the roots of our separation and of living from the heart.

It is in the Oneness that your true divine blueprint will make itself evident. This is one of life's great mysteries. By joining with the whole of life, you become the Greater Self, and there is only more of you to express love, wholeness, and the pure joy of being alive. It is in this Oneness that you really discover what it is you came to create and to express. Your life's lessons will automatically be revealed because you have healed the separation between you and your True Self.

Please know that you are receiving *great* support to shed anything that seems to be holding you back from your pure and divine Self-expression. *The members of the Spiritual Hierarchy are definitely making themselves available, as they want so much to be joined by embodied Lightworkers who have surrendered to the Christ within and who can, therefore, serve in creating more love and joy in the hearts of all those who are still feeling burdened.*

The Earth is a wonderful place to test and to realize your mastery, but you must be *very* strong to become God-realized on this planet. The inner Christ must truly sustain an attitude of "Thy Will be done on Earth as it is in Heaven!" When we are no longer enmeshed in the web of co-dependency and the threads of separative belief systems are cut free, then the real understanding of Oneness begins to shine forth as an actual possibility. Once tasted, a true yearning is birthed in the flame of the heart, and the desire for Oneness begins to penetrate every action in your life.

Descending into Form

Trust in the Lord, and he shall give you
the desires of your heart.

— Psalm 37:4
(*The Holy Bible*, Lamsa translation)

You PROGRESSIVELY EXPAND into the consciousness of your fifth-dimensional Lightbody until the spiritual essence of your I AM Presence is fully integrated with your four lower bodies. The Christ Flame within your heart, in conjunction with the chakras, will increasingly transmit these new energies into the cells of your body until they are completely transformed into the Love and the Light of the Christ vibration. As the Holy Spirit *descends* more and more into whole of your physical being, you are simultaneously *ascending*, or reuniting with the consciousness of your I AM Presence.

It is the Holy Spirit, as the spiritual essence of Mother/Father God, that is going to ignite your heart with the power that it needs to fill every cell and atom of your body with the fire of compassion. You may become increasingly aware of your I AM Presence. You may start to feel how it is aligning you with the Light and Love of your full God-remembrance. You may sense your Presence as a force which is pulling you upward through the crown of your head. With the help of the archangels and your spiritual overseers, your beloved I AM Presence acts as the magnetic forcefield that will eventually lift you into your final ascension from the Earth.

YOU ARE LOVED BECAUSE YOU ARE LOVE.
THAT LOVE FANS THE FLAME WITHIN YOUR HEART,
HOLDS YOUR FORM TOGETHER, AND
BREATHES THE DIVINE INTO YOUR BLESSED BEING!

It has taken many lifetimes to bring us into the illumination of this moment. Our power is not in yesterday or tomorrow, and yet it is the result of all our past and future thoughts and feelings. Woody Allen once said, "The hardest thing about life is showing up!" If we just knew how to be fully here, living in and as the *Heart*, it would be the most ecstatic gift that we could ever give or receive. I truly know that the Holy Spirit must descend into the embodied self if we are to be incarnate for the Christ and as the Christ. We must prepare ourselves, therefore, not to *leave* the body, but to fully *enter* it.

Having been an Eastern disciple for many lives, I am now coming to realize what it means to be a Western disciple of the Christ. In the last thirty years, I have come face to face with many of the basic beliefs that I brought with me from other incarnations. Often this has involved traveling to a country where I was particularly locked into a system of beliefs or identities. It took many years for me to fully break from the deeply ingrained belief that I must serve an incarnated Master Teacher in order to become God-realized. I also thought that I must put my focus into an established religious system in order to tread the "right" path.

The idea that I can embody my own Master Presence and experience total Oneness with God within my very own heart has seemed, at times, to be an impossible dream. When I truly desired to start coming into a more conscious alignment with my own Spirit, then the limited self started naturally moving out of the way. All individuals have the opportunity for sustaining their spiritual empowerment in the material world and *on the physical plane*. Realizing God while sitting in an ashram or meditating in a cave is not enough for this cycle of our evolution. *We are being awakened so that we can bring God into the marketplace!*

Our involvement in the ascension process is not a passive one. If our heads are in the clouds and our feet are not upon the Earth, then the chances are that we are not realizing ourselves as divine *human* beings living in a manifest world. The Earth provides us with such a great challenge: to bring the golden-white Light Essence of our most radiant Self into the densest realm of our physicality.

YOU CAME TO EARTH TO LIVE OUT

THE FULL SPECTRUM OF YOUR DESIRES;

LET YOURSELF EXPERIENCE THESE DESIRES

WITH PASSION AND UNDIVIDED ATTENTION

UNTIL THERE IS ONLY THE LONGING FOR GOD AS LOVE!

People live and die without realizing their dreams. They often do not have enough enthusiasm or life-force energy and passion to really manifest their desires. It takes a lot of juice to make things happen. The victim always blames outside circumstances on his or her lack of success; the dreamer and the idealist wait for the perfect timing and setting; the lover waits for the beloved; and the mystic waits for enlightenment and union with God. These most common dreams are coming to a close within the hearts of many during the closing of this century.

This age is shocking us into reality. The *fear* of pain and suffering has created such a wall of separation between the real world and the world of illusion that we put our *outside* desires before our *inside* desires, and we forget: we forget how to just enjoy life, we forget how to love ourselves and each other, and we forget why we came here in the first place! We are at last finding what we have been missing all along: ourselves, and our own *true* feelings!

You are the answer to your dreams. You really *are* the love, the lover, and the beloved, and when you find the *true* you and God within you, all your true desires will be met. Every material plane desire can then be manifested more easily, either by you or for you. Every outside thing that you really want will find you! It just works that way. You become the magnet for your own dreams to come true. That is why you are here.

It has all been a great game that we created so that we could live as God in a manifest world. It is still wonderful here, if we realize how to play the game. The Earth is now in transition, and she is cleansing herself in order to usher in this new millennium. We are too. Sooner or later, we must stop creating any new karma for ourselves or our Earth. It is not necessary to judge oneself or others for past actions, but we probably need to keep our eyes open in order to see what part we play and what part we can heal in the collective unconsciousness.

We are always attracted to the areas where we can learn the most and be the most effective. Movies are a great way to view humanity's overall state of well-being. They are also a wonderful way to see where you fit into the world mind. If you are willing to take a supportive approach with your so-called *lower* self, you will move that much faster into balanced alignment with your *unlimited* Self. Any part of life which attracts you is for a very good reason. We are always balancing ourselves between polarities. If we eat food that is just *good* for us, there is probably a shadow aspect of the self that is wishing it could have a piece of chocolate cake. That shadow self will have to have its day sooner or later, and it could be that you will have to reincarnate just to have that chocolate cake!

You are a *free* spirit! That which does not support your real freedom will automatically become apparent to the insight of your heart. Look upon your life as objectively as possible. As you consciously begin to eliminate your unnecessary personal garbage, you will be calling forth your true life's purpose. Civilization has not trained us to live as free beings. Outer authorities do not usually want us to have control over our own lives.

The truth *can* and *does* set us free! It is one of the most empowering gifts that we can bestow upon ourselves in these challenging times. The name of the game, however, is *LOVE*. All forms of hidden fear—within the guise of judgment, resentment, grief, remorse, jealousy, competitiveness, anger, and greed, to name just a few — can be brought out into the open and released if we love ourselves and each other enough to release our shadow selves in a responsible fashion.

We can love ourselves free, and we can assist others in doing the same if we can remain powerfully present within the body as the Heart. This is one of the most fantastic challenges that we face. We can so easily lose our connection with the heart if we sink too deeply into an angry, wounded, or defensive position. Balance is the key. If we become too fixed, solid, or contracted in any area of our life or being, then we know that we have become temporarily bound by the illusions of the mind.

DO NOT BECOME ATTACHED TO YOURSELF AS A SPIRITUAL LIGHT BEING; YOUR SHADOW SELF WILL JUST BECOME GREATER!

Metaphysicians can become overly attracted to the non-physical dimensions where half-truths abound. For spiritual seekers, this is a very real hazard. When and if you see yourself becoming too involved in the formless worlds, forgive yourself, re-center in the heart and get on with your life. We are probably juggling more than has ever been expected of us in all of history. We are ascending into Spirit and descending into form simultaneously. We are preparing to embody our Higher Selves while we are continuing to live on a third-dimensional planet. We do not really know if the planet is going to *physically* shift, but we do know that we are all shifting into a new world consciousness.

ALL CHAKRAS MUST BE HEALED AND IGNITED FOR THE FIFTH-DIMENSIONAL LIGHTBODY TO COME FULLY INTO FORM; AND ALL CHAKRAS MUST BE UNIFIED WITH THE HEART FOR THE HOLY SPIRIT TO ENTER AND ALIGN WITH THE CELLS OF THE PHYSICAL BODY.

Being Real

"... you shall walk in your way with hope and your foot shall not stumble. When you lie down, you shall not be afraid; yea, you shall lie down and your sleep shall be sweet."

— Proverbs 4:23,24
(*The Holy Bible*, Lamsa translation)

We are no longer victims or oblivious children seeking to find a God to take care of us. We know that it is now time for us to fully accept our God-given dominion to be in charge of our lives and world. You are your own best friend and you are consciously or unconsciously aligned with your Christ-self, once you have sincerely made the call for your ascension or the call to live this life in perfect attunement and alignment with God.

As human beings, we have been trained for fight or flight because we have been living in survival mode. We have not trusted ourselves, each other, or the world. Our egos and our fears have prevented us from living as real human beings. Remember through your ongoing processes into the Greater Light that we are truly all in this together. No one has all of the answers or all of the pieces to the puzzle. Begin to create more trusting relationships where you know you can surrender to hearing each other on deeper and deeper levels. This will also enable you to have much more creative exchanges. We are really just learning how to create friendships which support our spiritual freedom and our empowerment in the manifest world.

As you look back on your life, you will probably discover that every person who has come into your life has been perfect for the "lesson" you needed at the time, and all of the experiences that you needed for growth were given to you without your conscious request. The truth is that you are forever living in the Oneness; it is really impossible to be spiritually separate. Love, however, cannot be fully known or experienced until the heart is free.

WE CANNOT ACTUALIZE PLANETARY TRANSFORMATION UNTIL WE REALIZE PERSONAL TRANSFORMATION.

Every day counts toward the building of this New Age. Once you accept living in the radiant splendor of your own heart, you will no longer want or need to *escape* from the suffering on this planet. You will reach the point of no return and a part of you, even if it is not 100% of your consciousness, will never be able to go back to living your old life for any extended period of time. You will be here, but you will not be the same person.

I have so often asked the eternal question of Why am I here? Besides the intention to expand spiritually, the answer is simply *desire*. We are here because of our intense passion to create, to manifest, to complete karma, to ascend, to give and to receive love, and to serve. Some of us are even here to reach other planets and stars, whose inhabitants require that we first pass through the initiation of the heart — the initiation that the Earth offers all of her evolving inhabitants.

How is your life feeling to you right now? If it feels good, then the chances are that you are listening to that still small voice of guidance which is keeping you spiritually and physically in tune with your truth and your destiny. If you feel good about yourself, then you are being real and you are in the flow of God's Life in you and through you.

If you are apathetic, then you are in limbo. This is not really bad; it is just a difficult and confusing time which we all face in our

Earth lives. All feelings, even passivity, are a part of living in the ever-pulsing life-force of a water planet. Sometimes we can get frozen in fear: afraid to change, afraid to experience pain, afraid to die, afraid to grow old, or afraid to surrender in love. Fear can become a chronic disease that needs to be healed and loved free. The only way out of the house of fear is to go through the door of *fear* itself. Let yourself feel everything that is coming through your body to heal, and you will walk through that door with increased love, power and wisdom. If you can embrace all that is inside of you, then you will be at home inside of yourself. That is a great place to be on your ongoing spiritual path!

Psychic Opening

"Our gifts differ according to the grace given us. If your gift is prophecy, then use it as your faith suggests ..."
— Romans 12:6 (Jerusalem Bible)

WHILE RECLAIMING OURSELVES AS SPIRITUAL BEINGS, we begin to experience the opening of our higher chakras. These centers are often associated with certain psychic powers and as they develop, we see that "in my Father's house there are many mansions." The doors to these other worldly dimensions, or mansions, are opened very systematically. The keys are never given out prematurely, and sometimes they are not given at all. If someone appears to be psychically open but they do not have an open heart, then be assured that they are learning some lesson. Perhaps they have been a black magician in another life and they need to learn not to abuse their psychic powers in this incarnation.

Psychic clairvoyance, or *seeing* into the fourth dimension, is becoming relatively common-during these transitional times. Clairvoyance based on higher-dimensional seeing, however, is relatively rare because it involves a more expanded activation of the sacred All-Seeing Eye. This kind of seeing is generally quickened when there is a certain degree of balance between the heart, the throat, the brow, and the crown chakras. This balanced, energetic flow must be established before the Holy of Holies, or the Secret Place of the Most High, is activated within the center of one's head, where true alignment is made with the All-Seeing Eye. Only the Grace of God, however, can truly open this All-Seeing or "third" eye. Sometimes a Master Teacher can facilitate this opening. We can certainly do our parts in healing and balancing our human natures. It's my understanding that the third eye is generally opened when one's soul has contracted to use clairvoyance as a part of their service to the Divine Plan.

There are always good reasons for remaining veiled. Every chakra is very intricately related to your entire process of unfolding. These spiritual centers give off very precise energy indicators that are *read* and monitored by your own I AM Presence to determine your readiness for spiritual advancement and psychic unfolding. Although you may not feel ready, as I certainly did not in the 1960s, your Presence knows when and if you are spiritually ripe to open into a new level of consciousness. That first level is usually, but not always, the astral (or lower fourth-dimensional octave) of the Self.

Your I AM Presence works in Councils of the Christ Light with your guardian angel(s), your body elemental, and your own Ascended Master sponsors to determine how ready you are to spiritually take the next step. Your "Council" really knows best, so often psychic openings and powers are sealed for your own highest good. You will also be given many tests along the way to see how you use your gifts. Many times I have been so psychicallyopen that it almost took me into a psychotic state of mind. My sponsors have *watched* me now for years to see how I handle each new opening. A couple of times my extrasensory abilities were closed after only a few days, due to my inabilities to handle the energies. I am most grateful for their overseeing.

Since the lower self has dominated the human consciousness for so long, it takes some discipline and fine tuning to bring the still small voice of the heart (the thymus of the heart chakra), the Secret Place Of The Most High (the pineal gland of the crown chakra), the center of divine Will (the thyroid gland of the throat chakra), and finally the All-Seeing Eye (the pituitary of the brow chakra) into perfect alignment.

Lightbody Breathing and Meditation

"... He would grant you, according to the riches of His glory, to be strengthened with might through His Spirit ..."

— Ephesians 3:16

THERE IS VERY LITTLE PEACE in the world. If there is any peace, it must be within you. Meditation is an excellent way to experience peace with yourself and the world. As you learn how to align more and more with the Presence and Essence of God, that peace or still point of beingness begins to exude over into the whole of your life. True meditation begins to occur when the mind is no longer hindered by distractions. Each arising thought flows in and out of the mind until there is a steady, single-pointed stream of consciousness with no thought.

"Saints and sages and all those who want to live continuously within a Divine atmosphere of Love and Light often find themselves wanting to sever all bonds with the material, physical world. You have been given by the Christ for this next age and millennium new templates for mastery which did not exist in the old cultures and religions.

"The teachings of the Christ are being redefined so that they may be used by the present day initiate. We have given many in your world the foundations for these new teachings. Religions, World Teachers,

and avatars come to plant the seeds, which often do not flourish for hundreds or even thousands of years. In order for these seeds to bloom, they need to be nourished by those of you who are presently embodied. We, your spiritual overseers, will continue to help you in establishing a new reality in your world.

"It has taken nearly two thousand years for man to even begin to comprehend that he has been given the same opportunity to transform matter into Light and Light into matter, as did the Christ who came to teach man these basic principles of manifestation. You upon the Earth will work more successfully with these Cosmic Laws when you have cleared your minds and bodies enough to ascend into the higher levels of your own God-consciousness.

"You are presently receiving great assistance for accomplishing this from those of us who have already ascended. You are being given this support through guidance and increased energy. The true teachings of the Christ must now be brought into manifestation in order to establish the foundations for the dimensional shift that is fast becoming a reality upon your plane.

"As you continue to learn how to transform your physical bodies into their higher vibrational octaves, you will also learn how to receive your nourishment from the Divine Essences which support all life that is living in the Oneness. First you must understand the Law of Love, which is the natural order of being in the higher dimensions. Please remember that you who are presently awakening upon your planet have already accepted the challenges of living as radiant Lightbeings in physical forms.

"Instead of reaching 'nirvana' by taking your consciousness out of your body, you have elected to sustain this blessed state of union with God with your Spirit remaining in your body. That is the challenge of the fully-Christed estate. I taught you to live in the Peace of the Oneness. The Christ continued my mission and the mission of all God-conscious Beings.

"I enfold you in the Love, the Peace, and the Light of our victory in the Oneness. May you be continually embraced in the harmony which is the true and natural order of the universe in which we live."

— The Lord Gautama Buddha
through Julianne Everett
Mount Shasta, California

How do we now accomplish that which is being asked of us by the beloved Lord Gautama? How do we take charge of our lives in such a way that we are neither suppressing our feelings nor denying our higher capabilities to function as Lightbeings within what *appears* to be a third-dimensional world? Meditation can be used for breathing into the heart of the Christ Flame while aligning yourself with All That Is!

The following visualization and meditation may assist you in awakening your relationship to your I AM Presence. You might think of your Presence as one great and glorious interdimensional body of Light, filled with God's perfect Love, or you may visualize your Presence existing in tiers of Light which are each layered into their respective frequencies of color and sound. In this multidimensional visualization of the Self, each layer, or octave of consciousness, would vibrate with the chakra that acts as its spiritual control center. As with all meditations and visualizations, I would suggest that you give a prayer before beginning. Here is an example:

"Beloved Father/Mother God, Beloved I AM Presence, Ascended Masters, and Great Cosmic Beings: please add your Love and Light to my meditations, and make the following visualization a reality in the manifest world if that is in accordance with the Divine Will for my lifestream. So be it in God's most Holy Name ...

I AM that I AM!"

Please remember to do the following meditation/visualization while you are consciously *breathing* into every area of the body that is being activated. You may find it helpful to have someone else guide you through this exercise:

❤ *Visualize your physical body, your astral body, your etheric body, and all of the other levels of your multidimensional self tiered into increasingly refined layers of Light.*

❤ *See or imagine each of the chakras (spiritual control centers) connecting you with all of these multidimensional layers of the Self. Start at the Earth chakra, which is approximately 6–8 inches below the feet. Visualize this chakra and each subsequent chakra spinning in perfect accord with your "I AM Presence."*

You do not need to decide whether your chakras are spinning clockwise or counter-clockwise; simply affirm that they are going in the correct direction under the guidance of your I AM Presence.

❤ *Visualize each chakra, one at a time, vibrating to the sounds and colors which resonate with your Christ-self.*

Please do not project what you think the colors are supposed to be. Simply affirm that the *correct* colors are being activated for aligning you perfectly with your Christ-self and your I AM Presence. For the sounds, you may find it helpful to call in the dolphins and the whales and to let them assist you in the toning. They are very effective interdimensional helpers who are involved in tuning our bodies into their respective dimensional frequencies.

The dolphins align us with the higher sounds and the whales align us with the both the high and the deep tones. You may make these sounds inwardly until you are comfortable with making them out loud.

❤ *In accordance with the Divine Will for your lifestream, visualize each chakra being set free from the connections and cords that you wish to clear from your past. You can increase the healing power of this visualization by placing everything and everyone that you are releasing into the transmuting action of the Violet Flame.*

Be sure to check for cords in both the front and the back of your body. Do this exercise only if you are sure that you are ready to psychically disconnect from your past associations. If you do choose to sever cords from yourself to other people, you will be leaving psychic holes in all those involved. Be sure, therefore, to fill these holes with Love, Light, and absolute forgiveness, so they don't refill themselves with undesirable energies.

❤ *Always call forth the "I AM Presence," the Christ-self, the Recording Angels,[37] the Ascended Masters, and the archangels[38] to assist you in filling any remaining holes or vacuums with the Pink Ray of Divine Love and the Violet Ray of transmutation and forgiveness.*

Do this for everyone involved, whether they are deceased or embodied.

---

[37] Angels who record the activities of your soul and pass them on to the Keepers of the Akasha.

[38] Archangel Michael of the Sapphire Blue Ray can be invoked to assist you in cutting yourself and others free from psychic cords. Archangel Zadkiel amplifies the Violet Ray of forgiveness and transmutation, Archangel Chamuel amlifies the Pink Ray of divine Love and compassion; and Archangel Uriel releases the healing Ruby-Gold Ray of ministration and peace. Archangel Jophiel amplifies the Yellow Ray of wisdom and illumination, and Archangel Gabriel amplifies the Crystal White Ray of purity, resurrection, and ascension.

❤ *Please sustain an attitude of forgiveness and gratitude for those with whom you are severing connections. Breathing in and out of the heart always helps to keep the love flowing.*

Everyone who has come into your life has served you. Before attempting this kind of release work, you may want to find a professional healer who is familiar with clearing psychic cords from the subtle and physical bodies.

❤ *Visualize your chakras as perfectly aligned. Imagine a shaft of Diamond Light connecting you to all the layers of your multidimensional self. See this shaft of Light, which is also called your "Solar Spine," extending out from your physical spinal column.*

❤ *Extend this shaft of Light down through your feet, into your Earth chakra and into the core of the planet; then extend it out from your crown chakra and up into the Great Central Sun. Expand it to embrace the whole of your Self, whether you are seeing yourself as a singular point of Diamond Light or as a great Cosmic Being.*

❤ *When you feel in alignment with your "I AM Presence," then visualize all of your chakras and all of your bodies unifying with your heart in one sphere of golden-white Christ Light.*

This visualization will align your heart chakra with the Heart of the One Self by unifying it with all of the many dimensional expressions of your being.

Though I usually feel that meditations should be done in an upright position, I have found that this particular unification exercise can also be done while lying down. It is very effective to *unify* oneself before arising from bed in the morning and before retiring at night. Some of you are transitioning in and out of many different Lightbodies during the night. While lying down, the body often relaxes to such an extent that the Lightbodies can be deeply felt by your refined senses.

I CANNOT OVER-EMPHASIZE HOW IMPORTANT IT IS TO CONSCIOUSLY BREATHE YOUR SELF INTO YOUR HEART AND BELLY!

The etheric body, which sustains the blueprints of our third- and fourth-dimensional bodies, is important to include in this meditation because it contains so much of the encoding that we need for bringing the emotional, mental, and physical bodies into alignment with the Christ-self. It is also very important that we begin calling forth the blueprints of both the I AM Presence and the Cosmic Monad, so that the divine plan for the whole of the Self can be brought into our conscious world, mind, and body. This will also assist you in serving from your higher-dimensional Lightbodies.

Please note that much personal and planetary healing service is presently needed on the astral plane, which is the Earth's equivalent to the lower emotional body. As we become more conscious of how we can utilize the fifth-dimensional Lightbody of the Christ-self, we can safely enter into this realm and assist the angelic hosts in their work. Originally, the human, angelic, and elemental kingdoms worked together. Now, we are finding ourselves once again remembering how to invoke and even direct the angels to where they are needed in our lives and the lives of others. The "call compels the answer" is a cosmic law to which all the heavenly host respond. I find it most effective to invoke the archangels according to their rays, each of which represents a specialized service within the

Godhead. Footnote #38 on page 205 has more information on the archangels, their rays, and their services.

When the lower astral energies are cleared from one's blueprint, then the emotional body can become a guardian presence of pure Light. It becomes the lover, since it is the closest to the physical realm and therefore the most easily felt. When the emotional body is cleared, then this part of the self can be physically sensed as a kind of embracing energy, whose "arms" are constantly enfolding you with the essence of divine Love. This is how we literally *feel* God in the presence of others.

Since the first level of the etheric body holds the blueprints of your four lower bodies, it is intimately linked with your Recording Angel, who constantly imprints the Akashic Records with the spiritual progress of your soul. **When you are consciously living in harmony with the divine blueprint of your I AM Presence, you will become "whole-brained," meaning you will be living beyond the confines of the dual mind. As a whole body of enlightened cells, you will be living in Unity Consciousness, or Oneness. When you are in it, you will naturally be aligned with your true purpose in life.**

When the lower astral energy is cleared from the *planet's* aura, then the Earth can fully align with the Christ Consciousness grid, allowing her divine blueprints to release the encodings of the New Earth.[39] The astral plane can then expand into its higher destiny, which is to be a sustaining forcefield that is continually nourishing us with the essences of Divine Love and Light. By doing visualizations such as the one included in this section, Lightworkers are literally creating astral tunnels through the astral plane that are allowing shafts of Love and Light to penetrate the aura of humanity.

---

[39] This term is being used to define the Earth after she moves into the fifth dimension.

The Last Dance

"Call to Me, and I will answer you, and show you great and mighty things, which you do not know."

— Jeremiah 33:3

"Even heaven and earth will pass away, but my words shall not pass away."

— St. Matthew 24:35

I WAS JOYFULLY ANTICIPATING being a part of an annual week-long retreat at Stewart Mineral Springs, near Mount Shasta, California. My husband and I had house guests who were also participating in the retreat. I mention this because I think that my Higher Self chose to have Clare Heartsong, one of our house guests, present to facilitate the following experience.

The day before the retreat, I was feeling suddenly overwhelmed by an inexplicable anguish. I felt as though I was going to explode and let go of years of accumulated dross, but I had no idea what was really happening. I called Clare to be with me and I felt her huge capacity for allowing me to go through anything, no matter how extreme the emotional outpouring might become.

Beloved Mary, the mother of Jesus the Christ, appeared to my inner vision. She had on a pink dress. I asked her why. She said, "I want you to see me as a woman — not as the mother of Jesus, not as any kind of a Cosmic or Divine Mother — just as a plain woman filled with compassion for all of life. For that reason I am appearing to you in a simple pink dress."

She took me into the higher planes. There she bathed me with her Light and Love, stripping me down to what I thought was my very simplest self. Before I knew what was happening, she presented me to Lord Shiva. Then she left as quickly as she had arrived. Had not beloved Mother Mary introduced me to Shiva, I probably would never have been willing to go through the experience that followed.

Shiva appeared in a living body of intense light, holding an immense flaming sword — a blazing hot, life-sized sword. He kept saying to me over and over again, "I want it all: I want everything that you have ever thought or felt or believed to be the truth; I want every identity and every idea that you have ever had about yourself; I even want your I AM Presence, and your Ascended Masters and their retreats." This was really the last straw! My beliefs and every part of my mind and body were being sorely tested. Could I honestly give Shiva everything? I had to make a decision and I had to make it fast, or the moment might pass and never come again. Sometimes I felt as though I was dying. Clare held me as the purging continued.

I knew that this really was Shiva, and so I reluctantly acquiesced to his request. He came closer, bringing the flaming sword nearer my body. Suddenly, I could feel his intention. I saw that he wanted to put this sword inside of my body, starting at the base of the spine. I felt the searing energies of the flames tearing through my body. They seemed to be burning away layers of illusion as he thrust his fiery sword slowly through my torso, my heart, my chest, my throat, and finally into the pineal gland in the center of my head. I could not stop myself from bursting into tears. I cried so hard that I thought for sure I would be taken out of the experience, and then I thought no more.

Suddenly there was a great stillness and Lord Shiva disappeared. I dissolved into union with God; I never wanted to move again. This bliss was not an emotional one. The feelings were coming from such a great depth that they are really indefinable. All energy existed within an all-encompassing field of stillness. I was in the void, and yet all potential creation was pulsing inside of what was left of me. I no longer felt as though I had any kind of a body, and still I felt totally connected to some thread of consciousness which allowed me to remain present. If I was anything, I was just a point of Light. All identities seem to have been dissolved in Shiva's fire.

Quickly, I was transported to a cave in the Himalayas where I immediately entered a *spiritual remnant body*[40] that I had left there when I learned how to consciously sever my life-force in another incarnation. I felt as though I had been there forever. I was in rapture and in such a state of Oneness with God that I never, ever wanted to leave that cave. I truly felt immortality in every cell of my body. With this realization of the True Self, all fear of death left my bones. The tremendous sense of relief that swept through my being is beyond words. Finding this part of my self gave me a tremendous sense of cellular knowing: everyone truly is immortal! My ancient fear of death dissolved with this experience.

I really never wanted to leave that cave. I sat there in total nirvanic bliss, experiencing such union with God that I wanted to meditate forever and ever. I knew I had lived in this nirvanic state in another life and that I had chosen to consciously ascend into the spiritual worlds. The memory of passing over without really dying was imprinted in every aspect of my body-mind.

I was told that it was important for me to reintegrate this immortal aspect of the self into my present-day being. This was supposedly going to help me complete my service in the world. "What would ever make me want to return to the material plane?" Finally the answer came: "Love and only love will give you the desire to bring this immortal self into your body on the physical plane. *In order to complete your ascension, you must reclaim all parts of your total being; you must be brought into wholeness.*"

Although I could no longer see Shiva, I heard him saying to me with great laughter in his voice, "Oh, by the way, why don't you stop and visit the Ascended Masters El Morya and Kuthumi in Darjeeling on your way down the mountain?" It all seemed like

---

[40] A *body* whose memories remain as a part of the Akasha.

such a big cosmic joke. Shiva had just stripped me of everything, including the Ascended Masters and their retreats, and now here he was enticing me with this ludicrous invitation. It was, of course, a great teaching. He was telling me that it is all illusion and yet we are given the dominion to play in every world of form according to our desires.

After this, I felt very light and yet fully present as a feeling being. I don't know whether my immortal self has fully integrated into my heart and body, but I understand my assignment more. I know that I must descend into this body and world, and that this is the time of the Mother as well as the time of her Son. I would say that this is the time of the Christ as man as well as the Christ as woman. I am in the world in a new way. I am seeing everything and everyone for the first time. I am feeling everyone as myself, and yet I am simultaneously not anyone or anything. It is a paradox that must be lived if we are to be in the world and not of it.

Even in the paradise worlds, life is only a manifestation of Love and Light directed by conscious intelligence. We can play on any level that we choose. I *did* visit the Ascended Masters on the way down the mountain and I had the most joyful, intimate time with them that I have ever experienced. It is all as real as we want it to be, but if Shiva ever asks you to dance, just remember that it may be your last dance! Ultimately, we are only a spark of Divine Light and Love, so we might as well enjoy this incredible journey. Want to dance?

Cosmic Christ Invocation

I RECEIVED THE FOLLOWING INVOCATION telepathically from Jesus the Christ as he appeared to me in his radiant golden-white Cosmic Christ body upon the Sea of Galilee at Tiberias, Israel, in April of 1986. This invocation may be used to charge and align the physical, emotional, mental, and etheric bodies with one's own I AM Presence, which is manifested out of the Diamond Light substance from which all creation is born.

I FEEL from the HEART of my BELOVED "I AM" ...

I SPEAK and I LISTEN with the KNOWINGNESS

of the CREATOR that I AM ...

I live in THE LOVE, THE WISDOM, THE POWER and

THE JOY OF THE CHRIST ASCENDED.

As above, so below.

So be it in God's Most Holy Name.

"I AM THAT I AM!"

All that is CAPITALIZED within this invocation denotes a specific position of the fingers, hands, or arms because they are used in this prayer for charging your chakras and your physical, emotional, mental, and etheric bodies with Divine Light. When quickening your chakras with these sacred Rays, please place your index and middle finger of both of your hands in the *Victory* position of the Christ until noted otherwise. (I will refer to this position as the *Christ Mudra*.[41]) ✌

FEEL: *Allow your left hand to remain in a palm-upward position while doing the Christ Mudra with your right hand: Keep this mudra in place while placing the index finger of your right hand at your navel and your middle finger slightly below it.* (This charges the root chakra with the Crystal White Ray; the sacral, or second chakra, with the Violet Ray; and the solar plexus, or third chakra, with the Ruby-Gold Ray.)

HEART: *Place the index finger of your right hand slightly above where your rib cage ends at the sternum, and the middle finger right below it.* (This charges the thymus gland and the heart chakra with the Pink Ray. It also bridges the lower and upper chakras and awakens the Christ Gateway at the sternum.)

BELOVED "I AM": *The same two fingers are then placed over your chest, slightly above your heart.* (This charges the ninth chakra in the upper chest with the Magenta Ray, thus stimulating the harmonies that are contained within the full rainbow spectrum of creation, from red to violet.)

SPEAK: *Place your index finger in the hollow of your throat and your middle finger right below it.* (This charges the thyroid gland and the throat chakra with the Sapphire Blue Ray and it also stimulates the eighth chakra in the jaw area with the Aqua Ray of clarity.)

LISTEN: *Place your index finger in your right ear and your third finger just below your temple.* (This charges the "Secret Place Of The Most High" where one hears the voice of the I AM Presence.)

---

[41] *Mudra* is an East Indian word used to describe a specific hand position and/ or movement for aligning one with some spiritual virtue, such as peace, harmony, or courage.

<u>KNOWINGNESS</u>: *Same two fingers placed over the middle of your forehead.* (This charges the brow, or sixth chakra, with the Emerald Green Ray; and the crown, or seventh chakra, with the Yellow Ray.)

<u>CREATOR</u>: *Same two fingers now raised above the head while maintaining the same Christ Mudra.* (This quickens the relationship between the I AM Presence, the Christ-self, and its temple of expression, the physical body.)

<u>THE LOVE, THE WISDOM, THE POWER</u>: *Cross both of your arms over your chest at the heart.* (Allow yourself to totally FEEL how you are charging the Threefold Flame of your heart with the perfection of the Christ!)

<u>AND THE JOY OF THE CHRIST ASCENDED</u>: *Slowly release your arms, still holding your fingers in the Victory position, into a shoulder high, open-armed gesture of joy.* (This allows your human self to feel its union with your Christ-self and it aligns you with all of the facets of your multidimensional Self.)

<u>"I AM THAT I AM!"</u>: *In a large and joyous sweep, bring both of your hands together just slightly above your crown chakra in a palms-together prayer mudra.* (This aligns the left and right hemispheres of your brain and body. It also strengthens the multidimensional bridge that connects your Pillar of Divine Light[42] with your etheric spinal column, which contains the full spectrum of the sacred Rays that sustain your thirteen major chakras.)

---

[42] This *Pillar* refers to a column of Light that connects your physical body with your higher dimensional Lightbodies, and ultimately to Source.

Prayer to World Servers

Received on Easter, 1988, by Julianne Everett

To my brothers and sisters engaged in bringing the Earth and her people into the remembrance of their Divine heritage ...

Let thine Eye be single,
Lest thy world fall from Grace.
Let thy heart beat with purity,
Love's Eternal Self in thy embrace!

Become a conscious Living Flame,
Birthing the Christ for whom thou came.
Living the truth with every thought, word, and deed,
Saying "I AM THAT I AM," a vessel for thee.

For you, beloved, are the Light for the world
Whom God has sent for freedom's flag to unfurl.
Remember, remember from the Heart of the Sun,
The vows that you made for this victory to be won!

To live in the Peace and the Joy of the Son ...
In the Purity, the Harmony, and the Law of the One!
Thy lifestream to pledge its allegiance strong,
Thy goal of Ascension to be its song!

(continued)

To bring this Earth into its sweet Golden Age,
The Sacred Rays of God we now engage.
Into our bodies we anchor these Fires,
Transmuting all unnecessary desires.

Until at last we stand ...
Wholly ascended and free.
That is my prayer for the Earth and her people,
My ongoing pledge of allegiance to Thee.

To Thee, Oh God within all life, and to Thee, the beloved Ascended Masters and Cosmic Beings who are serving us so magnificently in bringing us ever closer to living the Laws of Love and Life as they exist in the realms of illumined Truth and permanent spiritual freedom.

⟡ BIBLIOGRAPHY ⟡

Burton, Robert E. *Self-Remembering*. Yorktown, NY: Joel Friedlander, 1991.

Eadie, Betty J., and Taylor, Curtis. *Embraced by the Light*. Carson City, NV. Gold Leaf Press, 1992.

Hicks, Jerry and Esther. *A New Beginning: Handbook for Joyous Survival; Abraham Speaks, Vol. V*. Boerne, TX: Crown Internationale, 1988.

Hurtak, J. J. *The Book of Knowledge: The Keys of Enoch*. Los Gatos, CA: The Academy for Future Science, 1977.

Johnson, Robert. *Owning Your Own Shadow: Understanding the Dark Side of the Psyche*. San Francisco, CA: Harper, 1991.

King, Godfre Ray. *The Unveiled Mysteries, The Magic Presence*, and *The "I AM" Discourses*. Schaumberg, IL: Saint Germain Press, 1935–1940.

Lamsa, George M. *Holy Bible from the Ancient Eastern Text: George M. Lamsa's Translation from the Aramaic of the Peshitta*. New York: Harper Collins Publishers, 1982.

Marciniak, Barbara. *Bringers of the Dawn: Teachings from the Pleiadians*. Santa Fe, NM: Bear & Company, 1992.

Michael, Arnold. *Blessed Among Women: The Birth, Life, Ministry, Ascension and Coronation of Mary, Mother of Jesus*. Westlake Village, CA: Gray Publications, 1986.

Milanovich, Norma. *We, the Arcturians*. Albuquerque, NM: Athena Publishing, 1990.

Morgan, Marlo. *Mutant Message*. Lee's Summit, MO: MM Co., 1993.

Sheehan, Patricia. "The Vision." Unpublished, 1993.

The Holy Bible, Authorized King James Version. Philadelphia, PA: The National Bible Press, 1947.

New Merriam-Webster Dictionary. Springfield, MA: Merriam-Webster, Inc., 1989.

❧ ABOUT THE AUTHOR ❦

Julianne Everett

In the 1960s, Julianne was spiritually awakened by the living presence of Jesus the Christ and Mother Mary. For many years, they trained her to reawaken the Christ that resides within every heart. Their teachings eventually began to reveal the mysteries of the ascension and its important role in our present lives. Julianne was also introduced to other Ascended Masters who are presently working with Jesus (as Lord Sananda) in initiating the heart into the Christ frequency. All of these radiant beings are in constant service to the Divine Plan.

Over the last thirty years, many spiritual experiences have led Julianne to embrace what she believes to be her primary service in this embodiment — to assist humanity in reconnecting with God through the heart. She feels that it is the Christ vibration within the heart that can shift humanity's consciousness out of separation and fear into oneness and love. From visions received during a trip to Egypt and Israel, Julianne was guided to write *Heart Initiation: Preparing for Conscious Ascension*.

Julianne holds a B.S. degree in Business Administration and an M.A. degree in Human Behavior. She has had additional training and certification in massage, rebirthing, nutrition, personal development, and psychotherapy, and has held a number of positions utilizing her skills in both healing and business. At present, Julianne facilitates personal and group alignments with the love, wisdom, and power of the Christ within. She invokes the Ascended Masters, the archangels, and the Elohim to assist individuals and groups in actualizing their full potential as divine human beings. Using the

Sacred Rays, the harmonics of sound, and the Diamond Merkabah, she provides a space which encourages people to *feel* their individualized and collective divinity. She travels globally, giving talks and facilitating workshops. She is also available (by appointment) for private work, which can be done in person or by telephone; if requested, these sessions are audio-taped. Julianne can be contacted by writing to her through Oughten House Publications, at the address shown on page 224.

❧ About the Publisher and Logo ❧

The name "Oughten" was revealed to the publisher fifteen years ago, after three weeks of meditation and contemplation. The combined effect of the letters carries a vibratory signature, signifying humanity's ascension on a planetary level.

The logo represents a new world rising from its former condition. The planet ascends from the darker to the lighter. Our experience of a dark and mysterious universe becomes transmuted by our planet's rising consciousness — glorious and spiritual. The grace of God transmutes the dross of the past into gold, as we leave all behind and ascend into the millennium.

❧ Publisher's Comment ❧

Our mission and purpose is to publish ascension books and complementary material for all peoples and all children worldwide.

We currently serve over fifty authors, musicians, and artists. Many of our authors express the guidance of such energies as Sananda, Ashtar, Archangel Michael, Saint Germain, Archangel Ariel, Serapis, Mother Mary, and Kwan Yin. Some work closely with the Elohim and the angelic realms. They need your support to get their messages to all nations. Oughten House Publications welcomes your interest and petitions your overall support and association in this important endeavor.

We urge you to share the information with your friends, and to join our network of spiritually-oriented people. Our financial proceeds are recycled into producing new ascension books and expanding our distribution worldwide. If you have the means to contribute or invest in this process, then please contact us.

⊸❧ Oughten House Publications ❧⊶

Our imprint includes books in a variety of fields and disciplines which emphasize our relationship to the rising planetary consciousness. Literature which relates to the ascension process, personal growth, and our relationship to extraterrestrials is our primary focus. We are also developing a line of beautifully illustrated children's books, which deal with all aspects of spirituality. To obtain a complete catalog, contact us at the address shown below.

     OUGHTEN HOUSE FOUNDATION,
READER NETWORKING, AND MAILING LIST

The ascension process presents itself as a new reality for many of us on planet Earth. Many Starseeds and Lightworkers seek to know more. Thousands of people worldwide are reaching out to find others of like mind and to network with them. The newly formed Oughten House Foundation stands ready to serve you all.

You have the opportunity to become a member, stay informed, and be on our networking mailing list. We will do our best to keep you and your network of friends up to date with ascension-related literature, materials, author tours, workshops, and presentations.

NOTE: If you have a network database or small mailing list you would like to share, please send it along!

OUGHTEN HOUSE PUBLICATIONS
P.O. Box 2008
Livermore • California • 94551-2008 • USA
Phone (510) 447-2332
Fax (510) 447-2376